Gaining Ground

Dramatic Landscaping Solutions
to Maximize Garden Spaces

Maureen Gilmer
Photographs by Mick Hales

CB
CONTEMPORARY BOOKS

Library of Congress Cataloging-in-Publication Data

Gilmer, Maureen.
    Gaining ground / Maureen Gilmer.
        p.   cm. — (The Contemporary Gardener)
    ISBN 0-8092-2777-0
      1. Landscape gardening.   I. Title.   II. Series.
   SB473.G5514   2000
   712'.6—dc21   99-25207
                                      CIP

THE CONTEMPORARY GARDENER

Other books in the Contemporary Gardener series:
Growing Perennials in Cold Climates, *Mike Heger and John Whitman*
Growing Roses in Cold Climates, *Jerry Olson and John Whitman*
The Landscaping Revolution, *Andy Wasowski and Sally Wasowski*
Gardening Wisdom, *Doug Green*

Interior design by Kim Bartko
Photographs by Mick Hales
Additional photographs by Maureen Gilmer: pages 13, 15 (bottom), 19 (top),
29 (bottom), 31, 42 (left), 45 (bottom), 46 (all), 53, 54 (top left and right), 90 (left),
106, 112 (left top and bottom), 117 (all), 120 (top left and right, bottom right),
139 (right), 144 (top left and right, bottom left), 148 (left), 152 (all), 162 (top left),
167, 171, 172 (all), 182 (top left), 184, 190 (bottom left), 194 (left); by Michael
Glassman: pages 28 (top left, bottom right), 30 (top), 86 (top, upper left and right),
180 (top and bottom left), 183 (top right), 192 (all), 198.

Published by Contemporary Books
A division of NTC/Contemporary Publishing Group, Inc.
4255 West Touhy Avenue, Lincolnwood (Chicago), Illinois 60712-1975 U.S.A.
Copyright © 2000 by Maureen Gilmer
Printed and bound in Hong Kong by Midas Printing Company
International Standard Book Number: 0-8092-2777-0
20 19 18 17 16 15 14 13 12 11 10 9 8 7 6 5 4 3 2 1

To Michael Glassman

Si monumentum requiris, circumspice.

IF YOU WOULD SEE HIS MONUMENT, LOOK AROUND.

Contents

Foreword

A good landscape is like an annuity, an investment in our future that grows and matures as we do. It provides us with shelter, comfort, and beauty for years to come. I feel it is important that my clients are very involved in the design process as participants rather than spectators. This allows them to develop a new appreciation of their surroundings and the nuances of the landscape.

Above all, design must be practical. Twelve years in construction makes me very aware of how the landscape is built, how it must be maintained, how people will use it, and how important it is to the owner's sense of peace and enjoyment of place.

This book is the embodiment of my work and my dreams. With everything in life so temporary and transient, it is essential we develop roots. These permanent and lasting landscapes are greater than the individual: they are a gift to the next generation. With that in mind, I dedicate this work to my daughter, Jordan. I know that as she grows, the gardens I have created will give her a sense of belonging and a living annuity she can claim for the rest of her life.

—Michael Glassman

Acknowledgments

I would like to express my sincere thanks:

To Michael, who made this book a reality. He spent incredible amounts of time sharing his work with me, both in discussion and in touring each site. Few know the days he spent preparing his gardens for Mick Hales to photograph, and in making sure Mick could find his way around town.

To Jeanne Fredericks, my accomplished literary agent, who so deftly turned the proposal into a reality.

To Anne Knudsen, for finding our proposal compelling enough to make it part of NTC/Contemporary Publishing.

To Kim Bartko, who, in search of highest quality, sought out a large-format photographer.

Michael Glassman expresses his sincere thanks:
To his wife, Kathleen.
To his mother, Elaine Glassman.
To his associates: Tom Phelphs, Mike Heacox, Annette Heacox, Lisa Shenck.
To his contractors: John Van Liefde of Masonry and Concrete; Robert Littlepage of Valley Hi Landscaping; Tom Lovejoy, landscape contractor; and Jerry Messineo of Swimming Pools.

Maureen Gilmer and Michael Glassman would like to thank these garden owners who generously opened their home landscapes for review and photography.

John Alexander	Ben and Edna McCoy
Giles and Cindy Attia	Mrs. Irma Moore
Richard and Carolyn Boje	Tana and John Moore
Peter and Norma Bollinger	Mr. and Mrs. Pigoris
John Budlong	Mr. and Mrs. Ramos
Grant and Lois Chappel	Tom and Linda Richards
Ed Clark	Gary and Michelle Sackett
Drs. James and Kay Drennen	Stan and Jan Sartor
Michael Duckhan	Gail Siller
Loren and Nadine Evinger	Jim Stubbs
Jay Feagles	Drs. Summers
Lisa Forrest	Derek and Kim Vanacor
Bill Heir	Dr. and Mrs. Wardel
Dr. Douglas Kay	Dr. Pat Wiggins
James and Cathy King	Dr. and Mrs. Williams
Robert and Sandy Lorber	Willard and Angie Williams
Mr. and Mrs. Markis	

Introduction

This expression has recurred in my mind throughout the writing of this book, because small, high-intensity landscapes are so detail oriented. There is no room for sloppy design or incompleteness, because what is neglected will invariably become an eyesore that you'll find more vexing each year.

> GOD IS IN THE DETAILS.
> —MIES VAN DER ROHE, ARCHITECT

God is in the details sums up in a single mantra the underlying reality of these gardens. There exists an almost religious sanctity in the work, a discipline that demands perfection on ever-deeper levels. It is as though the creative process becomes a ritual through which we cannot hurry, lest the end result be desecrated.

As our gardens evolve, so do we. In our twenties, we might have viewed the landscape on a superficial level, too active to appreciate subtleties. Our thirties usually begin an age of discovery in which we fall in love with the components of style and design. In our forties, we perhaps begin to understand the value of permanence and discover the shape and texture of quality. And our half-century mark opens the golden door of fulfillment, when all our experiences become manifest in gardens that are as unique as we are.

This is a book of maturity. It is a view of the garden primarily in terms of its livability—how it suits the needs and yearnings of its owners. This approach is strongly landscape architectural because it emphasizes the constructed elements, what we collectively call the *hardscape*. For it is this structure, these immovable elements, that are expensive, but so permanent and infinitely beautiful.

All the designs you encounter in this book are buildable. In most cases, they are not gleaned from palatial estates but from condominium complexes and tiny bungalow yards. The materials are plentiful in today's market, so you need not go to the ends of the earth to obtain what you see. Best of all, they are affordable—though many of the materials are indeed upscale, these are balanced with cost-effective alternatives.

Above all, the gardens are varied, as they should be; for the hallmark of a poor designer is the adaptation of the same plan in garden after garden. Sure, you'll see repetitive elements such as stone columns among these pages, but these have been a part of good architecture since ancient Greece and Rome. You will see a lot of water as well; no other element is so vital to our quality of life. The palette of plants is but for suggestion, embodying the applications in small spaces that may be accomplished by hundreds of similar but more hardy species.

Enter the realm of things tiny but delightful. Discover the satisfaction of perfectly designed outdoor space and how it enhances your overall quality of life. For no other improvement can bring you closer to natural living, and no matter how hectic or technological your everyday world, you may always come home to rest and renew in the garden.

CHAPTER 1

THERE IS NOTHING, SIR, TOO LITTLE FOR SO LITTLE A CREATURE
AS MAN. IT IS BY STUDYING LITTLE THINGS THAT WE ATTAIN THE
GREAT ART OF HAVING AS LITTLE MISERY AND AS MUCH
HAPPINESS AS POSSIBLE.

—SAMUEL JOHNSON, *UNIVERSAL CHRONICLE*, 1759

The Less-Is-More Philosophy

A Triad of Space, Materials, and Plants

LANDSCAPES, BE THEY URBAN OR RURAL, ESTATE-SIZED OR
little more than a postage stamp, share one fundamental purpose:
to provide an environment for people. These places and spaces
must meet our needs in every way, from issues of convenience to
more ethereal factors such as peace and inspiration. Design,
according to Michael Glassman, is the manipulation of place and
space to make it fill all the requirements of human life—privacy,
joy, celebration, relaxation, and, above all, the kind of inner calm
that only natural things can provide.

To begin to see the landscape as Michael does, it's important that you ground your thinking in the language of conceptual design. The concept is called many things by many people, such as a *big idea*, *overriding goal*, or *intent*. But to this designer it is *theme*. Michael has always been interested in theater, and his perception of theme in landscape is based upon the idea of stage set design. To create sets and scenery for a play, you must determine the setting of each scene in the script. Then the most important characteristics of that location are defined and reproduced in order to provide a definite and clear sense of place.

To understand the theme of the landscape requires a very well-defined idea at the outset. It is amazing to see how many novices as well as professionals fail to accomplish this, and as a result spend a great deal of time and money thrashing about in hopes that the end product will somehow work. But the truth is that without a theme there can be no characteristics, and without characteristics the choices and decisions of the design process become arbitrary.

Theme choice for each project varies because there is input from many sources, but in general it is a combination of personal taste, interior decorating schemes, exterior architecture, and site layout. Some of these can be changed and some can't. The key is found in the Serenity Prayer . . . the wisdom to know the difference.

THE OUTSIDE OF ANY BUILDING MAY NOW COME INSIDE AND THE INSIDE GO OUTSIDE, EACH SEEMS AS PART OF THE OTHER. CONTINUITY, PLASTICITY, AND ALL THE NEW SIMPLICITY THEY IMPLY HAVE AT LAST COME HOME.

—FRANK LLOYD WRIGHT, *THE LIVING CITY*, 1958

Space: Six Major Challenges of Small Gardens

Our perception of a location and its size is the true definition of space. A space may be defined in tangible terms that establish clear limits of an area through physical boundaries. A room in your house is defined primarily by its four walls, which undeniably limit movement. Gardens can be like rooms, and garden space, small or large, is also defined by physical barriers. For example, a courtyard is defined by fences or building walls that without question set boundaries. All that exists inside these barriers is part of the space.

Space can also be something quite intangible—little more than a feeling that a place is different. Often this is a purely aesthetic quality that by its fundamental character defines the nature or existence of the space. The term *open space* is used to describe an amenity of undeveloped land integrated into residential neighborhoods for aesthetic benefits. Nothing but the unmowed wild grasses establishes this space as separate from the surrounding neatly trimmed and watered parkways and home lawns. There is no physical boundary, but what exists inside the realm clearly defines it as a distinctive space.

Another aspect of intangible space is that which we see but cannot occupy or control. Sometimes this is referred to as *borrowed space*, which is an important quality for smaller gardens because every square foot of ground is precious. Visual space can be borrowed by enhancing what we see outside the limits of a landscape, provided it is an aesthetically pleasing view. Hilltop homes with tiny lots but huge views are the most common example. But when no off-site opportunities exist, we may use wall trellage designed with carefully contrived perspective to fool the eye into believing there is space where none exists.

There are six major problems that occur again and again in preexisting home landscapes that involve the definition, size, and quality of outdoor living space. When remodeling, these can be corrected and improved through changes in grade, materials, and, most important, integration of interior with the outdoors to create a larger, higher-quality space. In newly constructed homes, there is less need for correction and more emphasis on spatial organization in early planning stages to maximize living area both tangibly and visually. Understanding these weak points and how to solve the problems they present is the most important aspect of landscape design.

Problem 1: The Fishbowl Effect

Ever feel as though the entire world is looking in on your back yard? Maybe it's just the nosy neighbor's second-story window that affords a full view of your most intimate outdoor spaces. Either way, privacy is a growing problem in high-density living conditions. It can seem downright impossible to find in small gardens.

Screening and enclosure are crucial to the sense of privacy. The feeling of being separated from the world outside is one of the most fundamental and ancient goals of garden design.

Lack of privacy has emotional consequences. There is little chance of ever feeling separated from the world or discovering the complete lack of self-consciousness that sets us all free from society. The religious mystics of the deserts who lived like hermits amidst the endless reaches of emptiness knew the value of separation and how it enriches the contemplative life. More and more we seek to remove ourselves and return to nature through gardens, and these should be created strictly to nurture our raw, overstimulated senses.

Unless privacy is reestablished in the small garden, there can be no place for renewal. Achieving it is the greatest challenge for urban designers, and the solutions are specific and effective if applied to each site individually and each owner personally.

Problem 2: The Cliffhanger Effect

One of the most common challenges of smaller home landscapes is the tendency to chop them up into tiny spaces barely large enough to be livable. This fracturing is often due to differences between the elevation of the floor indoors and

Living space had to literally cling to the edge of this home built on a very steep site, where there was no hope of finding an inch of level ground to meet the sliding door threshold. Wood deck is one of the most adaptable to extreme conditions.

the ground outside. With limited area, the ability to reconcile this disparity requires some really creative, carefully designed details.

The finish-floor elevation of a house is simply the elevation of your floor. If your house is on a concrete slab, the finish floor may be just a few inches above the surrounding ground plain. Most houses, though, have an elevated finish floor to allow for basements, plumbing, wiring, and forced air ducts underneath the finish floor. Depending on local conditions, some communities are forced to have abnormally high finish-floor elevations to allow for flooding or high groundwater. On hillsides and split-level lots, the ground plain on one side of the house may be far below the finish-floor elevation on the other side.

The old expression "The whole is greater than the sum of its parts" applies to conditions related to this disparity between finish-floor and ground-plain elevations. Under these conditions, there is no way to link indoor and outdoor spaces into one contiguous whole that increases useful area exponentially. This difference is often compensated for by the constructions of all kinds of steps, from concrete to wood or masonry; but steps do not increase the whole, they simply connect the parts. This finish-floor peccadillo is second on the list of problems because it has a greater impact on spatial relationships and usability by humans than any other environmental factor.

Problem 3: Dysfunctional Layouts

Have you ever watched the traffic patterns of your household? Are there certain connections or movements you follow day in and day out? A perfect example is the path from your bed to the bathroom, or from the stove to the dining table. You really notice this in the wear patterns of a carpet. Some parts still look new, while others are compressed and slightly different in color. These are the daily repetitions that define how we live and move within the spaces of our house. In smaller homes, the intensity of this use is multiplied because there are fewer options for getting from point A to point B.

The same minimum dimensions used by architects inside a house are applicable to the exterior spaces, yet so often these are either ignored or unknown when a garden landscape is laid out. Sometimes this is because a builder is working toward a minimal level of completion before the house can be sold, and he doesn't want to invest one penny he doesn't have to in the site. At other times it might be that someone conceived of the idea without thinking about the criteria that control the sizes and relationships of spaces.

There are many common problems that, if ignored, spell dysfunction in a landscape. But when satisfactorily addressed in an aesthetically pleasing way, the result will be both satisfying and highly functional. These are some of the most common sources of poorly functioning landscapes:

- *Pedestrian connections* are the logical links between doorways of the house and outdoor uses, which in smaller spaces may be short and challenging if there are many constraints. They may fail to directly connect a spa or play area, forcing

users across lawns and planters. Connections to a utility yard or garage have special criteria to allow garbage cans and other equipment to be moved through with ease. Worst of all, the connections might fail to link living spaces such as the patio or lawn to the house, effectively separating them from people indoors.

- *Usable area* is space that you require to spend time outdoors in comfort. Successful areas require a certain minimal square footage for dining, lounging, or simply gathering when there are more than one or two people involved. These should be directly linked to indoor spaces to maximize opportunities for a fully integrated small home landscape.

- *Comfort zone* describes the quality of usability and is somewhat subjective. Small gardens offer little room to move around in and few alternative seating patterns; so unless the space is adapted to a degree of comfort, people will go inside for shade or for protection from the cold. The locations and form of the usable area should be created with the user's enjoyment as the primary criterion in order to ensure that the space is pleasant in as many seasons as possible.

Problem 4: Too Many Styles

Have you ever looked at a house and landscape and sensed that something was wrong, but you just couldn't put your finger on the problem? You're not alone. Millions of homesites are suffering a sort of multiple personality disorder in which part

The landscape for this Spanish-style stucco mansion was drawn from the traditional Moorish symmetrical courtyards of the Old World. Planting, paving, wall and gates, and the tile fountain are all appropriate elements that complement the architecture.

of the milieu doesn't match the other part. It's not hard to see the problem in an extreme example such as a postmodern house with a white picket fence and a cottage garden. This is likely a result of a homeowner who loves the gardens in *Country Living* but is inspired by the futuristic buildings in *Progressive Architecture*. One does not match or complement the other.

When you are working with a tiny garden, the emphasis on integration of the garden with the facade of the house cannot be overemphasized. There is little space to use subtle allusions or hints of connections. You must know what you are trying to achieve stylewise, and achieve it in a clear, consistent manner. Otherwise, neither house nor garden will project any definitive character at all.

There are two approaches to a coordinated, holistic home and garden integration. If the house has no apparent architectural style, such as a typical postwar tract house, then the door is open to establish a style and retrofit the building facade to be as complimentary as possible. There are limitations to how far this can be pushed; after all, there's no way you can turn a California bungalow into a Boston townhouse without practically rebuilding it.

More direct house and landscape style relationships might include a stucco-and-tile Mediterranean home with a semiformal garden that historically matched that architectural style. The Boston townhouse should have a garden that reflects the sophisticated urban New England preferences. Even a rustic wood cabin will call for a rustic, half-wild cottage garden.

Problem 5: Too Many Materials

In the small-space landscape, every inch is scrutinized microscopically, compared to larger landscapes, which are seen as though you were looking through a wide-angle lens. A proportionate amount of attention must be paid to the details in small

MICHAEL GLASSMAN

I have seen many homes where interior integration of spaces is totally lacking. One room is done in oak furniture, the other in cherry, and a third in mahogany. The carpet color and texture changes from room to room. The periods change, too, with French provincial here and Asian down the hall. For a place to be beautiful and well designed, it should at least show a continuity of color and materials in order to become fully integrated indoors and out.

spaces, no matter how insignificant they seem at the outset.

The most profound elements that integrate a landscape are the materials. They include paving, fences, walls, structures, and other constructed elements that bear similar hue, value, and texture. When the right materials are chosen, they all flow together into one environment. These in turn must work with the interior finishes of the house, as well as the exterior detailing of the building, for the whole to come together effectively.

In such a microcosm, landscapes created piece-meal will appear chopped up, confusing, and disorganized. In small spaces, there is little room to vary without purpose, because the risk of losing the thread of continuity is ever present. The preexisting problems occur most often where consecutive owners of a property have left their own mark on the place in the form of individual improvements accomplished over time. Ultimately, the key to remodeling such gardens is to emphasize simplicity and logic without sacrificing too much variety and interest.

The power of repetitive elements can be seen in this long, narrow city lot, where the overhead pergolas function like bookends on either end of a very simple pool. Although there is a lot going on in this landscape, it retains its classical simplicity—which is key to drama, particularly after dark.

ABOVE Set in a sea of mondo grass, this well-manicured Japanese black pine in its antique pot is a feature you can move around. Such sculptural plants are ideal subjects for nightlighting.
RIGHT Attention to detail in this landscape means that each square inch of this tiny composition is important to its overall success. In a tiny seating area barely 8 square feet (³/₄ square meter), the Buddha, bonsai trees with their decorative pots, and the ceramics combine with bamboo to present in miniature all the elements of a much larger garden.

Problem 6: No Focal Points

If we return to the notion that the landscape is like a theater set, then the next step is to see the performer as the focus of the scene. The audience sees the actor, in costume, as a component of the set, which illustrates how the overall picture is crucial to successfully convincing the audience that they are indeed in the time and place of the story.

This analogy is key to successful landscaping on a small scale. There must always be a focus for the set, just as the great landscape architect André Le Notre created a point of convergence at Versailles. In fact, this whole concept is at the core of the historic Italian gardens, in which Roman sculptures were the primary element, with the landscape seemingly designed around them.

When working in close spaces, there is no distance to use as Le Notre did, and there are surroundings that we cannot simply ignore, as their very presence spoils the illusion of the theater. Streets, houses, utility poles, and dozens of other intrusions can destroy the magic of the set. Therefore, we must control the perception of the person in the garden by forcing the attention to certain points.

Fine art is an ideal vehicle for controlling the perception of the garden. Sculpture, water features, architectural salvage, and antiques provide the opportunity for the feeling of grand vista within a small garden. These become inward-facing gar-

If You Do It Inside, You Do It Outside

Small gardens are simply outdoor rooms. And while we feel confident in decorating our interiors with carpeting, draperies, furniture, and art, once outside many people get lost. It may be that while interior improvements can be done relatively cheaply under a "paint and paper" approach, things you do to the landscape must hold up year-round in all sorts of weather. When it comes to plants, these improvements also take time to look good, often requiring many years—and such investments in money and time make people nervous.

It may be that plants are the major stumbling block; but as you will see in these chapters, small-space design is strongly devoted to permanent construction. Yet plants constitute such an enormous palette of color, form, and texture that unless you have a working knowledge of a good number of them, you really can't design well with them. But most people can pick up a package of paint chips or a wallpaper sample book and move right ahead in confidence.

To help you become better acquainted with the similarities between interior and exterior design materials, consider these parallels that will help you make the proper connections. For everything you do inside, there is a corresponding exterior treatment outside.

If you only have a small living space, it's a crime to deposit the garden hose in a prominent location. But if there's no alternative, stow the hose in an artistic ceramic pot. The pot must be heavy enough so it won't wobble or tip over as you coil the hose inside it. An outer finish that complements the landscape integrates the pot completely into your design.

Inside Walls	Outside Walls	Inside Floors	Outside Paving	Inside Art	Outside Art
wallpaper	brick	carpet	tile	painting	painting
mirror	concrete block	linoleum	concrete	sculpture	sculpture
faux finishes	stone	wood	deck	mural	mosaics
paneling	fences	stone	stone	tapestry	bonsai
paint	paint			artifacts	artifacts
lattice	lattice	Inside Windows	Outside Views		
tapestry	vines	drapes	trees	Inside Plants	Outside Plants
		shutters	hedge	hanging pots	hanging baskets
		screen	grillwork	small trees	potted plants
				foliage plants	vines

dens by containing a high concentration of interest and art that reward the wandering eye with treasures set against a vine-cloaked fence or hedge of black bamboo.

Each small space should be designed to draw all eyes to the point of interest. Without such a focus, the landscape would simply be a garden filled with plants rather than a three-dimensional cultural experience. This also allows the opportunity for surprise when the art is subtly nestled among the plants, peeking out from beneath the camellia or hanging shrouded by Boston ivy on the wall.

The danger in this approach will always be the potential to create a hodgepodge of tacky decorations that make the landscape look more like a yard sale than a crafted museum-like environment. Perhaps the key is to envision the patina of age on all things. A new back yard may appear to rise up out of the past with its Jerusalem oil jars and its Moorish grillworks when they are framed in the appropriate setting. Just as we can be eclectic with our interior decorating motifs, combining meaningful things and beautiful ones in the garden becomes an intimate expression of ourselves, our lives, and our loves.

This is a simple palette consisting of brick with a degree of color variation and an earth-tone olive stain for the wood fence. These muted materials make the planting stand out with its vivid greens, a variety of foliage textures, and splashes of floral accent color.

Materials: The Glassman Palettes

At the prestigious Bel Air Hotel above Beverly Hills, a tremendous amount of attention is lavished on even the smallest detail. Whether it is the entry carpet, the window trim, or the exotic fresh flower arrangements in the dining room, every color and texture is perfectly coordinated into a seamless, beautiful whole. This is preconceived by the interior designer, who presents to the hotel owner exactly what paint, fabric, and carpet colors will be used. These final choices are called the *palette*.

Michael Glassman pays extraordinary attention to the palettes used in his landscapes. He describes the garden palette as "a grouping of textures, colors, and materials that combine the house and its style with that of the landscape." Although plants make up a part of this palette, it is the hardscape, the constructed elements, that are the most critical issue because they are the most expensive and long-lasting.

Choosing a good palette for a landscape requires attention to a number of issues that are both aesthetic and practical. The palette cannot be chosen arbitrarily, because it must be integral to either the inside or outside of the house. If the house exterior has colors, textures, or materials that can be used, these become the springboard for assembling a palette.

Sometimes the house exterior offers nothing to work with, and the landscape will be arranged to play down the building and play up the spatial design. In this case, the palette is chosen according to how the interior is designed and furnished, in order to enhance the connections from indoors to out. Paint, floor coverings, and even furniture can become the basis upon which exterior materials are chosen.

When all else fails and there is virtually nothing to work from, then it's time to create a palette from scratch. You may already know what character you are looking for and have an inkling of which materials appeal to you. Most people do. In this case, you should invent a palette that exhibits the colors and textures that suit your personal taste. However, over time it's best to improve your interior style so that both spaces will evolve together in the same direction so that the entire homesite is integrated.

A Palette to Die For

One of Michael's latest projects illustrates just how detailed the application of a particular palette can be. He was faced with an uninteresting, average tract home owned by a professional woman who was a world traveler. She wanted the garden to express her love of far-off lands on the Pacific Rim that were lush and tropical yet understated, avoiding those sudden splashes of color so popular in Florida.

Michael decided on a contemporary palette that was muted and natural, with greens and sea tones evocative of those coastal jungle environments. Water would be a primary theme, with the very small space dominated by the plants and the pool with its creative edge treatments.

His palette would be dominated by primary paving of Indian slate, a multi-colored stone hued into various-sized rectangular tiles that are set precisely, the lines of the mortar joints contrasting with the marbled hues of rich wine red, lavenders, and gold. The secondary, lower-cost paving would be textured concrete with an integral green color for a faux finish that gave it an interesting irregular, heavily aged look. Sufficiently different yet still connected to the Indian slate in value, this paving added interest, particularly at the many abrupt grade changes in this space.

The pool would blend with the paving by complementary waterline tiles of the pool that were textured gray-green with black mottling. To further carry the palette into the swimming pool, he arranged a green-black plaster color that would lend an olive tint to the water and make it more reflective at night.

This was then carried into new hand-painted wood doors finished in an old Balinese-inspired print with yellow and green accents. The furniture he chose to complete the scheme was itself primary and tertiary. The primary furniture is handmade teak, with a small vignette of a rust-colored wrought iron finish speck-led to mimic old bronze, with coordinated cushions.

Because the house color was a light cream color and produced intense glare within his composition of subtle earth tones, he had the rear walls painted a shade of gray-green that was inspired by shades found in the Indian slate. Other embell-ishments for the space included a bamboo fence that combined with South Seas artifacts and with exotic planting to create a feast for eye and soul, all within a 30-foot by 30-foot (9-meter by 9-meter) common tract house back yard.

Other Concerns for Material Choices

Purchase price is certainly high on the list of concerns, because every project has a budget that dictates which materials are realistic within the financial constraints. Materials generated close to home are most affordable, because shipping of masonry and other heavy products can sometimes exceed the cost of the material itself. Always ask about shipping charges when pricing materials. Fortunately, small-space design requires just small amounts of materials, allowing you the opportunity to explore more expensive choices than would be the case with a larger landscape.

On a more practical level, you must choose materials that can realistically be built and finished the way you imagine. Michael considers these issues as well when preparing a palette, as they are crucial to whether his landscape is buildable.

Installation costs are critical because some kinds of materials require the skill of experienced masons, who tend to charge higher fees for their services. Any bricklayer can build a concrete wall, but it takes a real craftsman to veneer that wall with flagstone or cobblestones. These kinds of stone have irregular shapes that must be carefully fitted together to produce a quality product. Their thicknesses also vary, which means that even more attention must be paid to the setting bed depth to produce an even, flat surface. Similarly, the average concrete contractor can pour a slab, but not all of them can provide your project with attractive hand-scored joints or exposed aggregate surfacing.

A subtle combination of textures and hues blends paving, waterline tile, and small spillway tile into a single coordinated palette.

Availability of some materials can be surprisingly spotty when it comes to quarried stone, particularly if it is imported. It can also be a serious consideration when working with teak, mahogany, or clear heart redwood because old-growth and rain forest woods are becoming more difficult to find every day. There must be enough of the material to complete your entire project, because if you run short or parts of the order are damaged, you may need to order more.

Longevity applies to the material's ability to hold up under sometimes severe weather. For example, landscape architects redesigned the casino strip in Reno, Nevada, using a material called Idaho quartzite. When first delivered, it was a beautiful glittering silver-gray. After one year, the surface quality had so faded that none of that original opulent sparkle remained, and the entire project had dulled to a tone more consistent with run-of-the-mill gray concrete. No one had taken into consideration the effects of heavy foot traffic and weather, so that material that cost $10 a square foot (.09 square meter) to install ended up looking like a $3-a-square-foot (.09-a-square-meter) concrete job.

A Hierarchy of Materials

Cost is always the deciding factor when choosing materials for landscape construction. Even the largest budgets have their limits, which requires us to develop strategies to get the hardscape built without sacrificing the overall quality of the design. When it comes to materials selection, the strategy is to use high-quality choices in the intensive-use or closely visible areas. Then, in less-scrutinized parts of the landscape, we may choose one or more secondary materials that either mimic or complement the more expensive ones. For example, we may use an expensive stone wall in the front garden, but in the rear yard it may be matched by a less-expensive textured concrete block in the same color range.

In most landscapes, the greatest construction expense is paving, which is used on patios, walkways, and driveways. The cost for even an economy paving is considerable, so let's look at this material and how you can stratify its applications within a landscape.

It is rare to find a Glassman landscape that features just one paving type. Michael is known for combining a hierarchy of pavings, each according to its purpose and position. Understanding how these relationships work tells us how they are combined sensibly and for the right reasons. The art of choosing paving is to use variety without causing the landscape to appear disjointed, having too many different pavings with no visual or functional relationship to one another.

One of the most common reasons for using a hierarchy concept is cost. Very high-quality paving like Indian slate, bluestone, and granite is expensive to buy, ship, and install. But we so appreciate every aspect of smaller spaces that a high-grade material can become a major element in itself, just as an antique Persian carpet is more a work of art than just floor covering. So rather than settle for a

---

MICHAEL GLASSMAN

Don't force the hardscape to be unnaturally complex. Keep the circulations and spatial layout simple, simple, simple, so the user is not frustrated by an enforced meander that may not be logical. Then lend the casual character by the type of material, such as flagstone. Planting should overlap and soften the corners and edges with its own rangy character and form.

less-expensive option for the whole site, we can use two or three types of paving.

Primary paving is the most highly visible through windows and especially where it intersects interior flooring at doorways. Often the indoor floor can flow to a beautiful primary paving in a seamless transition linking interior and exterior into a single space. This is particularly important at large doorways such as sliding glass doors and French doors. Primary paving should be more refined in color and texture. It must be easy to walk on and has to hold up under heavy foot traffic. These areas not only experience a high level of traffic, but they are where outdoor furniture will be placed. Paving materials should be dense, resist staining from outdoor dining accidents, and resist scratches from furniture. Above all, paving must be friendly to both bare feet and stiletto heels.

Secondary paving can experience a high degree of traffic as well, but not in terms of outdoor living. More often, this paving provides the vital connections between high-profile living spaces and functional points such as utility yards or garage doors. They are sized and chosen to accommodate garbage cans, wheelbarrows, lawnmowers, or furniture. Secondary paving is lower in cost and less refined than primary paving, while remaining durable enough to resist damage from utility equipment. It will be visible from primary paving areas, so the two must complement each other, making the transition points appear more natural. Secondary paving is most often concrete, though it may be upgraded with techniques such as surface color, acid finish, exposed aggregate, and imprinted patterns.

Tertiary paving experiences only occasional traffic. It is a courtesy paving that allows a pedestrian to access parts of the landscape when it is too wet to walk on lawn or soil. This may be as simple as individual flagstones set out as steppers through shrub beds. It could even be brick set right on the ground without benefit of edge, setting bed, or mortar. Even pathways of packed decomposed granite fall into this category, for they can provide fine access in all sorts of weather for a very low cost. The dangers with tertiary paving arise when it is subjected to effects of freeze-thaw and soil heaving, which may demand resetting or leveling from time to time. However, these casual surface treatments can look the most natural of all surfaces in gardens that are long on plants and short on the signs of human hands.

A large, natural homesite required three different surfaces using primary, secondary, and tertiary pavings. Primary paving at the front entry was composed of exposed aggregate poured concrete edged with brick: excellent for partygoers wearing high heels and slippery-soled shoes. Secondary paving was Nevada moss flagstone laid out on a concrete slab with mortar. This is an irregular surface that was used to traverse a private valley behind the house and worked well with wheelbarrows and casual traffic. The tertiary paving was the same flagstone, laid out on a bed of decomposed granite, which was amenable to all the ups and downs of the topography and offered alluring pathways into shaded tree groves.

TOP Indian slate, a perfect example of primary paving, here is cut and milled to geometric perfection and laid in a precision patchwork of color and shape. **BOTTOM** This driveway has been treated as both secondary and tertiary paving. Cantera stone tile was used at the front door patio. Secondary paving includes the dark bands in the driveway, which are dark tinted concrete imprinted with a stone surface texture. Tertiary paving includes the light fields of the driveway, composed of rough finished concrete stained with acid after it dried and cured.

Small gardens require plants that are proportionate in both overall size and the size of their individual leaves. Here the small leaves of Japanese maple combine with maidenhair fern, azalea, and English laurel, illustrating how much diversity can be achieved in just one square foot (.09 square meter) of space.

FLOWERS HAVE AN EXPRESSION OF COUNTENANCE AS MUCH AS MEN OR ANIMALS. SOME SEEM TO SMILE, SOME HAVE A SAD EXPRESSION; SOME ARE PENSIVE AND DIFFIDENT; OTHERS AGAIN ARE PLAIN, HONEST AND UPRIGHT, LIKE THE BROADFACED HOLLYHOCK AND SUNFLOWER.

—HENRY WARD BEECHER, *A DISCOURSE ON FLOWERS*, 1867

Plants: Botanical Tribes

Plants are the perishable living element of every landscape. They are not static, but continuously grow and change with the seasons. Volumes can be written about choices and applications. But to view plants as a landscape architect is quite different than viewing them as a horticulturist, who loves them for their cultural qualities. In environmental design, plants are seen as form and mass, color and texture, with an ability to change and modify a space to make it better suited to human beings.

To understand the associations of plants to style, it is helpful to view them as tribes. Plant tribes, just as human tribes, are groups that are alike, that belong together. But within the tribal affiliations there can be further divisions that establish in even greater detail the individual plants that should be incorporated

DIE WHEN I MAY, I WANT IT SAID OF ME BY THOSE WHO KNEW ME BEST, THAT I ALWAYS PLUCKED A THISTLE AND PLANTED A FLOWER WHERE I THOUGHT A FLOWER WOULD GROW.

—ABRAHAM LINCOLN, 1842

into landscapes of certain styles. In a way, this is stereotyping; but as you will discover, plants may belong to different tribes, depending on how they are grouped or shaped. For example, a boxwood shrub allowed to grow naturally might belong in a woodland garden, but since these plants are nearly always clipped into rigid hedges, they are more often associated with formal gardens.

Most residential landscapes will fall into one of these tribes—but do not allow this to control your hand too much, because there are always new and dynamic combinations that may defy classification yet are intensely beautiful. The following plant lists are those most often used in Glassman landscapes, but are in no way exhaustive. They are but examples of representative species that epitomize the tribe's character. Literally thousands of other plants exist that make more heat, cold, wet, and dryland alternatives that may be far better suited to your immediate microclimate.

Mediterranean Tribe

This style, originated around the Mediterranean Sea, was perpetuated by Arabs, Greeks, and Romans and carried by the Spanish to the New World regions with similar climates. Where climates are too severe for Mediterranean plants, citrus and pomegranate may be grown in large terra cotta pots.

Trees that offer great promise include the new fruitless olive tree variety 'Swan Hill.' More recent varieties of crepe myrtle (*Lagerstroemia indica*) may be used as a single-trunk standard or more broadheaded multiple trunks. Citrus is always appropriate, even if planted in large terra cotta pots to allow sheltering during winter.

Tall Mexican fan palms (*Washingtonia robusta*), Italian cypress (*Cupressus sempervirens*), and a blue foliaged species of eucalyptus are primary examples of trees suitable for the Mediterranean palette.

Roses of all kinds are appropriate, as are high-profile climbers such as passionflower and the very tender bougainvillea. Dwarf pomegranate shrubs (*Puncia granatum 'Nana'*) are most versatile, and *Nerium oleander* is among the fastest-growing and most colorful privacy screens. Too rarely seen is *Arbutus unedo*, the strawberry tree, grown as a shrub—it also makes a fine standard tree for small spaces.

And on the smaller scale, both the upright and prostrate forms of rosemary are star performers. French and Spanish lavenders, plus *Acanthus mollis*, the Greek inspiration for Corinthian column capitals combine with *Pennisetum setaceum*, the most common and perhaps best ornamental grass.

Asian Tribe

Here we gather together the specialties of the Far East, where the garden is a quasi-religious experience. The plants are classical and well adapted to most climate zones and can be used in many other tribal combinations due to their intense color and wide variety of forms.

Japanese maples (*Acer japonicum*) are seen in many of the gardens in this book in their natural form and in the shorter, bronze cutleaf varieties. Camellia and azalea, certainly no strangers to the West, are brilliant floral displays that combine with the maple to produce the great woody triad of shade gardens.

The mugo pine (*Pinus mugo 'Mugus'*), if regularly clipped, is highly drought resistant. A true Asian natural is heavenly bamboo (*Nandina domestica*), which is actually not bamboo but grows in a similar tall, thin shape. Weeping cherry trees and crabapples are available in many forms and make a brilliant showing each year, as do the saucer magnolia clan.

Among this tribe are the bamboos, most often *Phyllostachys nigra* with its mahogany-colored canes. Mondo grass (*Ophiopogon japonica*) and liriope species and hybrids are highly adaptable grasslike plants that serve as groundcovers, foliage around rocks, or edging. The variegated forms are delightful for bringing light to dark shade.

ABOVE The Asian garden is populated with familiar plants such as this blooming saucer magnolia (*Magnolia soulangiana*), azaleas, pruned cypress, and mondo grass (*Ophiopogon japonica*). **BELOW** Blooming organ pipe cactus is intensely exotic. Like many other plants that are too frost tender, growing in containers allows them to dwell indoors for the winter.

Tropical Tribe

Just because a plant looks exotic does not mean it is very frost tender. Many plants evocative of the far-away South Pacific equatorial jungles or other warm climates, if placed in another garden tribe, would present a wholly different character. Use this list for alternatives.

Instead of	Use
Torch ginger	*Kniphofia uvaria* (red hot poker)
Orchids	*Canna* × *generalis* (canna lilies)
Elephant ear	*Acanthus mollis* (bear's breech)
Clivia miniata	*Amaryllis* or madonna lily
Bougainvillea	*Campis radicans* (trumpet creeper)

Most of these plants are soft, herbaceous sorts. Bananas make great foliage; they rarely produce fruit but will take surprisingly low temperatures and grow like crazy to replace their frost-killed parts the following summer. The South American angel's trumpets (*Brugmansia spp.*) behave much the same way. Canna lilies are great choices that can be placed in pots to bring indoors—new varieties offer some really exotic colors, but smaller flowers than the old white ones.

Roses, boxwood hedges, and topiary are the most characteristic plants of the formal garden. Though they are frequently dressed up with seasonal color, evergreens ensure that a garden retains its geometric beauty under a blanket of snow.

Formal Tribe

This garden is one of control, inherited from the Romans by the French, who carried the concept of the clipped parterre to incredible proportions. Formal gardens promise to be neat, tidy, and forever stylish.

This style, with its geometrical forced plantings, is headlined by species of privet (*Ligustrum*) and the boxwoods (*Buxus*), which are the most common hedge and topiary plants grown today. We also find the bonsai styles of Italian cypress (*Cupressus sempervirens*) and a host of junipers trained by growers into classical shapes. Evergreen pear (*Pyrus Kawakamii*) and Firethorn (*Pyracantha coccinea*) take the lead with espaliered shrub-trees that are trained to cling to vertical surfaces. Roses finish the play list when used in tree form, particularly the weeping China roses with their small but plentiful leaves and flowers.

English Tribe

This group is quite large and encompasses a number of styles that fall under cottage gardens, English gardens, and country gardens. What they all share is a love of color and flowers over all else. They are heavy on perennials, although very colorful shrubs and trees are equally appropriate.

Favorite trees that take to small landscapes include the goldenchain tree (*Laburnum anagyroides*) and both redbud species of *Cercis*, which offer charming fall

ABOVE Generous borders filled with blooming perennials are what make the country garden so charming. This same effect can be created in small spaces as well, using plants that are smaller, yet equally interesting.

LEFT Serbian bellflower (*Campanula poscharskyana*) is one of the best small garden groundcovers that blossoms well in shade. After blooming, it may be cut back to a light green ground-hugging mat that will remain for the rest of the summer.

The Birth of Topiary

The ancient Romans were fastidious bathers in a time when baths were not common in Old Europe. They built great structures for ablutions at Bath, England, and at various sites throughout their empire. In the Roman house, built around an open courtyard where the water source was featured, the daily activities were carried on in the open air. The use of fragrant oils derived from common herbs was part of the postbathing ritual.

The Romans wished to scent their entire living space with the fragrances of these essential oils. Their gardeners would frequently trim these woody perennial herbs to release the oils to evaporate in the courtyard air. In such enclosed space, this was a remarkable experience that could be enjoyed well beyond the Mediterranean climate of their homeland.

Over time, the regular shearing became an art form with the goal of helping plants retain their beauty, and the Latin gardener's name *toparius* was given to this new craft of topiary. Eventually, topiary work was done to any kind of plant that could be sheared well, such as boxwood, whether it was fragrant or not. But in our modern gardens we may return to the root of the topiary art, that of releasing scent, by planting sage, rosemary, and lavender close to living spaces. Then, with scissors in hand, we too may share in the age-old Roman art of scenting our gardens with herbal aromatic oils.

color as well. We find old-fashioned flowering shrubs such as lilac, bridalwreath spiraea, forsythia, hydrangea, and flowering quinces. Virtually every annual and perennial is included, with special emphasis on large flower spires of delphinium, hollyhock, liatris, and penstemon. Above all, wisteria vines and sweet scented jasmines combine with roses for a huge plant palette that makes choosing much more difficult than growing!

Wild Tribe

They are the creatures of the woodlands, the meadows, the stream canyons, and mountains, where plants in their most natural environment evoke the wild places we all love. It is always recommended that choices include an abundance of locally native species to create a well-adapted back yard version of wild plant communities.

Coast redwood trees (*Sequoia sempervirens*) are seen in many of these gardens as background and screen due to their propensity to grow tightly together and the lovely color of new growth. Under a tree canopy of deodar cedar (*Cedrus deodara*), oaks, maples, birch, and pines grow the dogwoods, though a new disease is threatening many species. On the shady floor of these forests and groves grow the rhododendrons, sweet scented daphne (*Daphne odora 'Marginata'*), columbines, wild violets, trillium, and other wildflowers. Ferns are limitless, with emphasis on maidenhair and the giant chain fern (*Woodwardia fimbriata*). There are also creeping red fescue and other ornamental grasses with Shasta daisy (*Chrysanthemum maximum*), corn poppy (*Papaver rhoeas*), and black-eyed Susan (*Rudbeckia hirta*).

The Triad Revisited: Space, Materials, Plants

We have explored the three fundamental aspects of attractive landscapes that incorporate a degree of livability characteristic of the gardens in this book. Failure to apply any one of these three will result in an incomplete garden, one that denies either aesthetic sense or personal need, or simply refuses to grow.

There must be enough space in the right location to make the landscape fit you. There should be an appropriate exposure, enclosure, and protection from the elements. Most important is that the garden space connect with the space inside your house so that you experience an environment that feels larger than the sum of its parts.

Choose materials wisely so that each inch of tile, paver, fence, or wall is as good as it can possibly be. Go beyond the old dog-eared planks and explore the many layers that make up the constructed parts, because if it is to be beyond good, to be your monument to beauty and botany, it must be superior. This may mean more travel to specialty suppliers, but in the long run you are assured a uniqueness that is a pure reflection of self in landscape.

Small gardens do not have infinite room for plants. They require only a handful sometimes, so these must be the most beautiful, interesting, and varied subjects you can find. Avoid the plants you know, and seek those you don't know but are drawn to by their uniqueness. Most important, hunt by size, because the greatest tragedy to befall a "needlepoint" garden is for plants to grow well beyond their space and spoil a carefully designed composition.

Take chances. Reject monotony. Imagine. Make your landscape something more, something that extends from your undefined essence channeled through preference, experience, and memories. Let your architecture speak in silent messages; and if you don't like its language, change it. For even the most average house on an average city lot can become, with a few dollars and a good design, a tropical paradise, your villa on the Riviera, Rome revisited, or the familiar hardwood forest of your childhood. Such is the magic of design, such is the sanctity of the landscape, and such is the art of it all.

A mature old tree leaning into a niche in the architecture allows the beauty of the forest-floor garden to flourish in shade. Maples, ferns, azaleas, babytears, and impatiens combine to create a lush microcosm of the wild.

CHAPTER 2

HOUSES ARE BUILT TO LIVE IN, AND NOT TO LOOK ON,
THEREFORE LET USE BE PREFERRED BEFORE UNIFORMITY.

—FRANCIS BACON, "OF BUILDING," 1600

Tract Home Transformations

Never Settle for Ordinary Again

ONE OF THE THINGS WE HAVE LOST IN RESIDENTIAL HOUSING OVER the past few decades is individuality. In the first half of this century, most homes were built by individuals on lots, and the house expressed the architectural preference of that owner. In some old neighborhoods, there is a remarkable assortment of styles, from Tudor to Spanish, colonial to modern.

The postwar American baby boom created an astounding need for housing. People were nesting and creating new familial life in the wake of wartime death and destruction. Families wanted the proverbial house with a white picket fence, but their youth limited their finances. The demand proved to be affordable housing, and to achieve this degree of economy there had to be a more efficient way to produce single-family homes quickly.

What emerged were builders who reorganized to build entire neighborhoods at once, not just one custom house at a time. Land in cities was too valuable for these young families, so the builders moved to the yet-undeveloped outskirts that would become American suburbia. Optioning large pieces of land, the builder proceeded to subdivide it as a tract into individual lots and roads.

Then he would have from one to five different modest wood frame or masonry houses designed, and often built models of each to aid in sales. To increase profits, the houses shared the same materials and style. Once a prospective buyer chose a model and a lot, the house was built. As a result, these tracts of houses tended to bear uncanny similarities at first, but over time the uniformity was reduced by remodeling, new facade or paint, and landscaping.

Hence the term *tract house* describes a home that offered little architecturally but served the needs of postwar families. As the cities expanded, the suburban land value rose and often exceeded by far the value of the unremarkable house.

Tract housing continues to occur across America, and today more families own their homes than at any point in our history. The newer tracts tend to be far less spacious, and some are so tight there are just a few feet on either end of the house to connect front and rear yards. In some cases, what is called a *zero-lot-line* condition allows a house to be placed right on the property line so that there is only one side available for side access.

Another example of this monochromatic approach to housing is the planned community, where the entire tract is designed to produce an integrated whole. This is actually the reverse of the postwar condition, for here the continuity of architecture and building color is strictly regulated by the community association. Only the rear yards that are out of sight from roads, trails, and open space may be adapted to the owner's wishes.

NOBODY WANTS A HOUSE OR A LANDSCAPE THAT LOOKS LIKE IT CAME OUT OF *THE STEPFORD WIVES*. EACH OF US DESERVES TO HAVE OUR OWN UNIQUE STYLE.

—MICHAEL GLASSMAN

Monotony and Mediocrity

Living in a tract house is a struggle against the monotony of the neighborhood and the mediocrity of the architecture. But one of the benefits is that these homes usually sit on sizable lots compared to those of modern tracts. This is a bonus that allows the owner to enjoy two environments of equal livability.

One of the ways to change this is to remodel the house. A second way is to remodel the landscape so that the improvements aren't in the dwelling, but in the environment in which the dwelling resides. This technique can turn the house into a virtually invisible entity hidden behind plants and garden art. It also allows the design of the interior to flow outdoors in a continuous fluid space that integrates both conditions. This emphasis on the landscape changes the character of the house from simply a dwelling to a holistic living environment.

The Mechanics of Sound Attenuation

The day will come when man will have to fight merciless noise as the worst enemy of his health.

—Robert Koch, *Conservation Foundation Newsletter*, 1910

Sound is one of the most insidious influences on our quality of life. It's invisible and has no mass or form, yet it is ever present in cities and suburbs. Freeways and other high-traffic areas are the greatest sources of continuous urban noise. Planners understand this and have developed ways to attenuate, or mitigate, noise through planting.

There are two methods of sound attenuation. The first is deflection, which is how freeway sound walls work. These very tall masonry walls that line freeway edges along residential neighborhoods bounce the traffic noise back toward its source. The second technique is absorption. Barriers of trees and shrubs act as insulation to catch and hold much of the noise so that far less is heard on the opposite side. Absorption occurs indoors as well, because an empty room bounces sound off walls, while a furnished one absorbs it into carpet and upholstery.

For sound attenuation plantings to be most effective, they must be located as close as possible to the noise source, not the living space. The farther back the barrier, the more sound is able to go over the top. Barriers must also be very dense, with low shrubs giving way to tall trees. The thicker the barrier, the more sound it can absorb. Evergreen plants are preferred because deciduous plants have no absorption ability when barren in winter.

Profile: From American Tract to Contemporary French

The house was the epitome of the featureless 1960s one-story tract house, low and rambling with virtually no architectural details to work with. Fortunately, the new owners shared sophisticated tastes for clean, contemporary styling with luxurious materials and finishes. In this way, Michael's new clients compensated for what the building lacked with some well-defined ideas of their own.

The large lot fronted on a quiet, tree-shaded residential street. It was set way back from the curb so there was absolutely no entry experience whatsoever. You had to walk up the driveway to find a little "trailer-sized" entry sidewalk.

Michael's design goal here was to create an important entry from curbside so that guests knew where to park and so that the front door was much more prominent. When you have a house with a monotonous roof line and a tiny front stoop, there's nothing to invite entry. And when there is so much entirely usable space to work with, there are rare opportunities to create a grand entry.

This solution involved a series of entry experiences, beginning with two matched pilasters close to the curb for a luxurious Beverly Hills–style entry gateway. This yielded to a nice, wide, elegantly curved walkway directly to the front door. To break up the continuous roof line, columns with an overhead arbor made it far more visible and offered a sense of arrival.

It is interesting to note that no two of the three elements—door, arbor, and gateway—line up. This is part of a *feng shui* principle: when too many portals line up, the energy from the interior is allowed to flow out. However, it's also good design because the dynamic of asymmetry provides more interest when the original space offers no relief in terms of topography or existing plant materials.

One side of the lot is adjacent to a high-traffic arterial boulevard. Fortunately, there was already a good sound attenuation barrier planted that cut off the view of the road and absorbed some of the noise.

ABOVE The original entry door and stoop, typical of so many tract houses. The smaller the entry, the less money needed to be spent on nonliving spaces by developers. But they always forgot that guests often arrive in pairs, and sometimes more, and that means that in this case, only the first person has any hopes of being out of the rain while waiting for the doorbell to be answered. When guests arrive, they should have ample parking, well-defined access to the house entry, and a comfortable place to wait. **ABOVE RIGHT** What was originally an obscure doorway becomes a grand entry with two basic techniques. First the doorway was framed with columns and an overhead. Then the stoop was extended from a tiny pad to a quarter circle of accent paving. The result is an elegant, contemporary formal place of arrival. **BELOW RIGHT** This is the visitor's view of the house, which offered no clue as to how to reach the front door—and even that was difficult to pick out. The recessed entry was closet-sized and was lost in the long, low profile of the house. This presented the biggest problem in the front yard.

MICHAEL GLASSMAN

You must separate modes of transportation. Use driveways for cars and walkways for people. It's not only unattractive, but unsafe to force visitors to walk up a driveway to your front door. The front walkway should be at least 5 feet (2 meters) wide and never in a straight line, or it looks like a gigantic tongue coming out of a front door mouth.

BELOW A new walkway was poured to allow convenient access from guest parking in the driveway directly to the front door. Using hedges and creative landscaping, the driveway is more like a plaza, with garden art and the fence faced in a coordinated diagonal lattice that matches the grey paving and pilasters. Lattice offers easy training of vines and roses, which over time combined with the double fence adds dramatically to sound absorption potential. The attenuation planting is clearly seen, existing on both sides of the fence with evergreens such as deodar cedar (*Cedrus deodara*), coast redwood (*Sequoia sempervirens*), and Chinese elm (*Ulmus purvifolia*).

RIGHT A tiny rectangular swimming pool was jammed up against the far end of the lot, probably positioned to make it easier to enclose with child safety fencing that was never built. *Coping* is a term used to describe masonry used around the edge of the pool. These precast units were standard for all pools back then, and defined the radius of the corners. The waterline tile was simple sky blue, and the surrounding deck was plain, uninteresting concrete. Topping it all off was a functional but ugly diving board. The algae-green water illustrates a common problem with old pools: the green can become impregnated into the plaster of the inner wall, causing permanent discoloration even when the water is replaced and treated. **BELOW** Pools, just like a house or landscape, can be remodeled. This illustrates the simplest way, which is the equivalent of the paint and paper approach to rooms. No expensive structural improvements were done. The single biggest change here was elimination of coping units for a single cantilever style of pool edge. Exposed aggregate, which is easy to take care of and looks neat and contemporary, was poured into place. The waterline tile was changed to creamy white to match the fresh new plaster. Although the pool is still too small, at least it is now fresh and attractive.

The rear yard of this tract house exhibited all the characteristics of millions of homes across the nation: poor planning, total absence of aesthetics, and lack of quality outdoor living space. It was set off completely from the interior spaces as more of an afterthought than the largest part of the property.

The challenges were to:

1. Create a spacious patio for entertaining. All that exists is a very narrow covered porch on a concrete slab.
2. Provide some high-impact gardening opportunities directly next to the buildings. The need for color and beauty is obvious.
3. Devise a means of connecting the far-away pool with living spaces. In other words, make all the floating buildings and pool look like an integrated whole.
4. Solve the dilemma of the bare garage wall. One can either make it great or make it go away, but never ignore it completely.
5. Add style and elegance to a very tired yard. Nothing here offers a shred of style to work from, so a whole new aesthetic concept needs to be conceived based on the interior design character.

The trees just beyond the covered patio were so surface-rooted from lawn irrigation that nothing grew beneath them, and their location prevented any expansion of the patio. Although it is always difficult to recommend removing trees, in this case it was unavoidable. If the roses and perennials desired by the owner were to thrive, they would need pure, unobstructed sunshine as much of the day as possible. Once the trees were removed, the entire character of this space changed, as though the slate had been wiped clean, leaving Michael with a fresh canvas to work on.

The first order of business was to expand the surface of the existing patio to make it large enough to use for entertaining. Originally it ended just inches beyond the original wood posts, now replaced by Roman columns. The area was doubled in size, which allowed for two tables to be comfortably used for entertaining. The paving was surfaced with pre-cast concrete pavers to match interior floor tiles without the cost of ceramics. At this level of the interior finish floor, the doors may be opened out onto a new upper terrace, half covered and half in the open air.

Rather than leave the terrace wide, the transition to a new lower-level plaza space was enclosed to focus traffic down the wide central steps surfaced in blue-gray slate. These matched raised planters are constructed out of concrete block, sealed carefully on the inside and coated with stucco on the outside. The owners have carefully trained creeping fig vines (*Ficus pumula*) to the face of the wall. This gives the illusion of yet another perfectly sheared hedge when viewed from the pool area. The lower parterre hedges contain a matched pair of flowering cherries (*Prunus serrulata 'Kwanzan'*).

The upper terrace steps down via an extra-wide step to a lower plaza. The top of this intermediate step and the faces of all other steps are finished in a unique blue-gray ceramic tile that the owners bought at deep discount in an odd lot. There were only enough tiles to use as accents to highlight the steps and other special places.

The remainder of the project is paved in exposed aggregate poured concrete. Exposed aggregate is the most beautiful, versatile, and affordable alternative available to standard concrete slabs. Rather than leave the endless lawn between the upper terrace and the pool, a plaza was created that focused on a single large fountain in the center.

The fountain is constructed within a large, circular raised planter. This allows seatwalls to improve versatility and lowers maintenance. It is planted in trailing verbena and other flowers that change with the season.

The real classical elements, however, are the columns, freestanding at the four corners of the plaza. They stand in the lawn so no special planter need be created for the roses trained in a spiral up the columns. Eventually they will grow large enough to produce bountiful flowers that cover up the stark, flat tops. One could place wide bowls or urns on the tops as well in the future, as the roses change the overall effect.

LEFT Each of the raised planter walls is topped with precast concrete capstones colored to coordinate with the columns and paving. They are planted with sets of three matched white tree roses trained as standards, and below are *Dianthus* pinks and trailing verbena. **BELOW** This view of the plaza shows the placement of the columns in the lawn and the expansion joints in the exposed aggregate, which enhance the geometry of the plaza overall.

RIGHT Close inspection of the fountain shows the raised planter wall constructed of matched materials, white stucco and precast concrete capstones. The fountain itself was prefabricated and then placed in the planter, which had been wired for electrical outlets. In the foreground is an unobtrusive black lighting fixture that shines up on the fountain itself. There are similar fixtures at regular intervals all around the fountain for even lighting effects. The planter is filled with trailing verbena, ivy geranium, and blue lobelia, all of which are frost tender annuals replaced each year. **BELOW** The columns in detail show how uplights are recessed partly underground and shine up on the columns after dark, enhancing the shadows of the spiraled rose canes on the smooth surface.

The garage presented another design dilemma because it was highly visible, but offered nothing but a plain wall with a single, ordinary metal frame window in the stucco. As always, there was the option to try to hide or disguise a potential eyesore, but doing this with plants would demand far more space than this area could afford to lose. The other option was to find a way to make it attractive.

The decision was made to upgrade the structure, and here we find the whole gamut of tricks of the design trade. First is the transition zone from the main house to the garage, which was upgraded to make the two buildings appear as a single structure.

The white stucco wall of the garage provided a great opportunity to completely change the character of the building. The idea was to achieve a cottage garden look by adding new doors and dressing up the walls.

ABOVE The back door to the main house kitchen was upgraded with gray slate. The original fence was removed and a fin fence sided with ship lapboards was added to extend the house siding. A door was substituted for the old gate to give a more structural effect. The door was pivoted at a 45-degree angle for a smoother transition.

BELOW RIGHT This view from the upper terrace shows the new doorway, which (along with the existing window) was given green shutters to match those of the main house. The walls were faced with white lattice so that the roses could be trained up to the eaves.

The problem with training roses or other nonclinging vines to stucco is that you need many holdfasts to control the way the stiff rose canes should grow. It's not a good idea to puncture stucco indiscriminately, because water can enter the wall at each place. To protect the walls, white lattice panels were bolted on, and at each puncture the stucco was carefully sealed. The climbing tea roses have now ventured out across the eaves, where they will bloom, in season.

The final touch to the garage makeover was a tiny hedge-bound cottage garden, the feet of the boxwoods covered by bronze coral bells. It is brimming with topiary forms, flowers, and herbs. Two *Podocarpus gracilior* trees, trained into matched columns, frame the window, and behind them for contrast is a red-leaf Japanese barberry hedge (*Berberis thunbergii 'Atropurpurea'*). To soften the far end of the building is an accent tree, a multiple-trunk specimen of crepe myrtle (*Lagerstroemia indica*) to offer late-summer flowering color.

What was originally a very stark, white house to protect pool equipment became a decorative element in itself. Its door was also given a pair of green shutters, and the window decorated by a window box. It was originally accessed from the far side of the garage by a narrow concrete walkway, but this was removed to provide a more creative connection. Since it is not a frequently used path, precast concrete stepping stones were laid out to connect with the garage, and then to the pool area. The fence, previously visible beyond the lovely old grapefruit tree, is hidden behind a new hedge and redwood trees to buffer the roadway noise beyond.

A new wing had been added to the house that mirrored the mass of the garage, forming a U-shaped building mass. Beyond that wing is another space that was once part of the open back yard, but now has the addition of an abnormally wide side yard with a "bowling alley" shape. Since the new room opens to the area with French doors, it would be highly visible.

What emerged is a design in the French style of an exuberant garden of perennials and herbs, a sharp contrast to the semiformal design of the main landscape. Pea gravel saved money on paving but matched well with exposed aggregate.

What this garden exhibits is proof that 1950s American tract homes can be upgraded to the sophistication of Europe and high social style. Just because it's a ranch house doesn't mean you can't use Mediterranean fountains or Roman columns. Anyone can evoke the formality of a French chateau garden and enjoy an abundance of roses with the easy care of new varieties. A palette that is clean, fresh, and highly affordable combines aggregate paving with accent tile, precast square stepping stones, and pea gravel into a single contemporary composition.

ABOVE LEFT The little house became a charming focus of a garden area that was created to nestle it in lovely green sheared plants. **ABOVE RIGHT** The original house ended at the extruded hot water heater closet. A single walkway makes this enlarged side yard garden accessible. Rather than centering the walkway on the space, an offset layout allows a larger perennial bed on the side that is most visible from indoors. Note how the exposed aggregate paving edge in the foreground transitions seamlessly to the less-expensive pea gravel.

Overheads and Enclosures

Gazebos are examples of freestanding shade structures that also provide a weatherproof roof and a deck floor. This shape, compared to post-and-beam, is more expensive to build because the joinery is more complex and the hexagonal shape requires deeper, more extensive footings. One advantage to gazebos is that they can be easily screened in against insects, and you can add lighted ceiling fans under the roof for all-season comfort.

The single repetitive challenge experienced with tract homes is the lack of comfortable outdoor entertaining area. Paving is not enough, because to use the area at different times of day and night, you need some additional amenities.

Shade is one of the most precious commodities in hot climates. If there are no trees, or those that exist are insufficient to provide much cool space, then an overhead shade-giving structure is necessary. Most tract homes were built with tiny patios, hardly large enough for a table and chairs. But to maximize indoor-outdoor lifestyle, you need a lot more comfortable space for dining and entertaining.

Shade structures are either attached or freestanding. The attached structures are connected to the house or another structural wall for support and are considered an integral part of the building. Freestanding structures stand purely on their own and need not have any connection with a building.

A structure may provide an overhead that is weatherproof, which requires a full roofing system. Some simply provide shade, and the degree of shading provided depends on the density of the members. Arbors can also be designed with widely

spaced members that will depend on vine growth to offer shade. These take some time to fill in and must be strong enough to withstand the weight of the vine at maturity. For grapevines or wisteria, this can be considerable.

One of Michael's projects involved a simple tract house that desperately needed shade. Trees were out of the question because the large lawn was bordered by very large, mature specimens. Yet the back side of the house seemed too sparse and open to feel comfortable or intimate.

Two types of structures were used in order to accommodate an unusual condition. The house sat about a foot (30 centimeters) lower than the level of the rest of the back yard. This required an overhead that could function well on both elevations. One attached to the house shaded the portion of the patio that was at the finish-floor elevation of the indoor rooms. Another freestanding structure provided a comfortable shaded dining area. All around the patio are new planters to provide a sense of enclosure and to add even more subtle changes in grade.

Homes with modern window systems that are exceptionally tall or feature transoms present similar elevation challenges. These structures, if attached to the building above windows, must be far taller than the average, which requires much stronger posts and joinery. But the lofty ceiling creates a much more luxurious space beneath with enough clearance to hang fans easily.

During the 1960s, when wood decks became all the rage, overhead shade arbors were treated much the same as decks. The emphasis was on very big, solid members like those used for loadbearing decks, except that nobody walks on the tops of shade structures . . . most of the time.

One of the older problems we've inherited from these original overbuilt shade structures is dark wood stains. The tendency to go *au naturel* and stain everything brown made the overheads dark and oppressive. This absorbed so much light that the interior rooms became dreary. In nearly every one of Michael Glassman's shade arbors, the finishes are in light colors: cream, white, and warm and cool gray.

ABOVE LEFT This residence was composed of a separate house and garage. The space between them was lost and difficult to work with, but ideally located for a completely covered outdoor dining and entertainment space. What resulted was a spacious outdoor room walled on three sides and open on the fourth to garden and pool. **ABOVE RIGHT** Though the space inside the new outdoor room is darkened by the extensive solid roof, it becomes absolutely festive and luxurious after dark. This kind of room also lends itself to screen panels for climates where mosquitoes are a problem in evening garden use.

What would otherwise be a "boxcar" effect with the long, low ranch house becomes a study in diversity. The main shade structure is to the rear and is connected to the house at the lower elevation. The second structure is centered on a slightly elevated upper patio. The whole space is enclosed by a series of raised brick planters of varying heights that combine to interrupt the tendency of this arrangement to seem long and narrow. The raised planters are high visibility but low maintenance.

LEFT The new, nearly freestanding dining area provides plenty of shade when the garden beyond is in full sun. The small cross members allow maximum sky visibility—but when laid out on edge, the shading potential is increased when the sun is in a morning or evening position. Japanese maples in various planters help reduce the starkness of the structure without using vines. **BELOW** This airy overhead just fits between the tops of the windows and the bottom of the roof rain gutter. This kind of tight placement is difficult to achieve structurally, and the post behind exists because the adjacent wing is of too low a profile for connections. Glare from the far wall was reduced by fixing a grid trellis for flowering vines, again to avoid unnecessary invasions into the stucco. The paving is tinted and imprinted concrete. This composition with building color, arbor stain, and light-toned paving creates a very bright and luxurious dining area.

ABOVE This tract house was remodeled with new windows, French doors, a wood shingle siding, and a structure that provides welcome shaded outdoor dining in hot weather. Its components are still not overly large, and the design provides plenty of structural support for the balcony above without being oppressive below. **LEFT** A tiny tract house jammed up against a major river levee felt like it was in a hole, with no hint that a beautiful waterway flowed on the far side of the mound. Michael designed this structure to provide a shaded dining area underneath during hot summer days, but with a special bonus: one end of the arbor supports a "widow's-walk"–inspired elevated deck that offers a view of the river. **RIGHT** For rustic effects, the materials used in freestanding arbors can be bold and creative. Cantera stone columns support simple pressure-treated "peeler pole" round beams allowed to weather naturally. This structure does not offer much shade, but vines can increase the shade potential. But with such unique materials, it's a shame to cover them up in foliage. Note the small lighting fixtures subtly hidden among the beams.

Stains and Paint for Wood Fencing

One of the most powerful yet least-applied techniques of rendering ordinary wood (both old and new) more beautiful is the careful use of color. In most cases, sprinkler water will mar the base of virtually any wood fence, so coloring and recoloring it over its lifespan is crucial to long-term beauty.

Michael Glassman's favorite product is Cabbot's Bleaching Oil. It provides a warm gray color that is comfortably neutral for light overhead structures. It also makes new wood decks suggest the silvering that was so attractive when aged heart redwood was still in the lumber market. There are a number of ways to color or seal wood:

- *Clear sealers* are designed to extend the life of outdoor woodwork while leaving the natural color unaffected.
- *Semitransparent stains* protect wood and have a trace of color in them, but the wood is still quite visible beneath. They help lend character but do little to cover up.
- *Heavy body stains* contain far more color and do have a good ability to cover and protect. Unlike paint, these are still stains and do not peel. They make the best choice for woodwork that is in need of a facelift or to bring woodwork into the color palette chosen for paving and masonry or other aspects of landscape construction.
- *Paint* is often the only way to bring an aged fence or arbor back to some semblance of beauty without costly replacements. It covers so well that sprinkler patterns, mildew, or old paint or stain can be hidden in a single application. Paint will crack and peel over time as wood expands and contracts with the seasons. Paint is also a good choice for contrasting lattice or grid arbors applied to neutral-colored walls.
- *Faux verdigris* is a great treatment for wood lattice and grid arbors that Michael uses to give the impression of ironwork.

Profile: Planned Community, Planned Monotony

Modern tracts are often redefined under the more contemporary heading *planned communities*. In the 1960s, every tract house looked the same for strictly financial reasons—to keep the homes affordable. Planned communities are not only planned monotony, they are expensive monotony, too.

This kind of community imposes strict laws, called CC&RS (covenants, codes, and restrictions), to ensure that the public view remains as unchanged as possible. Therefore homeowner's associations charged with enforcement of the CC&RS must approve any project proposed in the neighborhood. Anything and everything seen from street, sidewalk, trail, or open space must comply. In this community, the front landscape is strictly controlled, but what you do out of sight behind the fence is your business. However, if a shade arbor sticks up higher than a 6-foot (2-meter) fence, and of course it will, the structure must match the guidelines.

THE FRONT OF THE HOUSE IS JUST A FACADE. BUT FROM THE FRONT DOOR BACK, IT'S ALL YOURS—SO USE IT. THIS IS YOUR PRIVATE SANCTUARY, AN ENVIRONMENT WHOLLY SUITED TO YOUR SENSE OF BEAUTY AND LIFESTYLE.

—MICHAEL GLASSMAN

Such was the case when Michael began work on this contemporary tract/planned community house. It was new and nothing existed outdoors, but inside was a rich palette of stucco and Saltillo pavers and earth-tone masonry slump block used for the fireplace and chimney.

The owners presented a laundry list of needs; they were two single parents who had married and now lived with a raft of children who needed a safe place to play. Similarly, the parents needed a place to get away from the perpetual frenzy of activity. Above all, it had to look good, because the back of the house contained large windows and sliding doors so the yard would be visible from indoors.

The palette would be wholly architecturally responsive, and the idea was to lend the landscape project a patina of age despite the fact that the whole community was brand new. To achieve this, the slump block, a very affordable masonry unit, would predominate. Paving would be cantera stone pavers shipped from Mexico, with their rough, slip-resistant surface and irregular coloring. Terra cotta would also be used as accent, and metalwork treated to an antique copper verdigris finish would be employed.

The layout of the spaces would be in quadrants. Off the kitchen would be a service quad, with a lovely stone fountain and iron overhead rose arbor set into a niche in raised slump block planters. Although the space was purely functional, this element would add an artistic touch.

This project illustrates one of the underlying approaches of Michael Glassman's work, which is an undying attention to every square foot of the site. It would have been easier to just create a simple raised planter, but a thorough approach and the belief that no space is unworthy of an artistic flair ensures that the view from the kitchen is important to those who spend a lot of time there. With so many children, there is little doubt that this is the most active room of the home.

ABOVE The long walls that define the perimeter of this back yard were preexisting, composed of ordinary earth-tone concrete block. To break the long run into smaller segments, evergreen creeping fig and deciduous Boston ivy were planted to provide leafy background coverage. A pair of salvaged stone fireplace surrounds were used to support a lovely antique finish cherub. No construction or special detailing, just artful arrangement. ABOVE LEFT Custom-made and imported from Mexico, the carved stone fountain is classically designed and fits perfectly into the cove in the slump block seatwall. There are no plants around the bottom (to keep maintenance to a minimum), but note the short trench grate drain to ensure no water is trapped in the enclosed area. Roses grow out of the planter into a custom-built steel rod trellis that sacrifices no light with its presence. BELOW LEFT The above-ground spa fits perfectly into its niche against a blank wall. Embellishments make it less visible and increase the sense of privacy. The small lawn is visible in the background.

ABOVE This view extends over the wading pool to show how it is placed between building and fence. It illustrates how the outside wall of the pool also functions as a planter so that new elevations can be incorporated into the landscape. However, for child safety, Michael added a small ledge just above the waterline as part of the wall—a hand hold for young, fatigued swimmers. The perimeter wall beyond is shrouded in vines and planted in exotic foliage that is highly visible but practically maintenance free. **RIGHT** Although the pool design keeps fun and children in mind, it is also a stunning feature for nighttime entertaining. The wading pool, elevated and integrated into the wall system, doubles as a waterfall and night-lighting feature. Michael custom-designed the turquoise antique Chinese, ceramic lighting bollard upon its carved stone base. The ceramic is perforated and at night bears a pattern of bright beads of light. Beyond, a verdigris green woven iron panel adds interest to the long fence line.

ABOVE LEFT The overhead structure here had to be designed and finished in keeping with the community regulations because it could be seen from the street, which is just beyond the rear fence. The paving is cantera stone tile, which is porous and slip proof, and tends to discolor with algae and moss to create the patina of age so desired by the owners. The vines are lavender trumpet vines (*Clytostoma callistigioides*), which are quite tender. But cold winter alternatives would include Virginia creeper (*Parthenocissus quinquefolia*) or scarlet trumpet vine (*Campsis radicans*). Note the unobtrusive lattice enclosure that disguises utilities that could not be relocated. **ABOVE RIGHT** One-of-a-kind pieces are affordable in small landscapes because space is limited. Michael designed this lovely gate to separate the active family pool area from a quiet and passive adult garden. The gate's art deco motif with a hint of the American Southwest was specially finished to give it an age-old look.

An above-ground spa is rarely a thing of beauty, but after a long day at the office there is nothing more soothing than a relaxing hot dip. To provide the harried parents with this welcome form of therapy, it was placed out of sight from indoors and disguised from the adjacent spaces by a curb-high planter, boxwood hedges, and verdigris lattice above for privacy without sacrificing light or air movement. Beyond is a small patch of lawn, just enough to provide a soft play space for the youngsters and pets.

This swimming pool is unique in many ways. Above all it is created to maximize space, jammed as close to the fence line as the CC&R setbacks will allow. Second, it is designed for children, with an elevated wading pool that spills down into the main pool. But even there the depths are minimal overall, and it is accessed by steps the length of the inside curve.

The most beautiful outdoor room of this landscape is reserved for the parents, who no doubt need to separate from the noise and perpetual motion of family life. Fitting snugly between an adult sitting room and the perimeter fence is a cool, shaded garden sanctuary with a beautiful antique iron fountain centered perfectly upon the plate glass window to make this space part of the interior experience.

ABOVE LEFT The great beauty of this space is in the constructed details. Slump block seatwall at right adds sitting areas without the need for furniture. Perennial rosemary (*Rosmarinus officinalis*) is spilling over the wall and adds both culinary seasoning and aromatic foliage. The base of the fountain is also quite low and wide, so it does not visibly sacrifice the sense of openness. The fountain is so ornate that it is a treasure when viewed from close up. Ferns can be grown in practically any climate if chosen properly. **ABOVE RIGHT** Most landscapes are designed to be appreciated outdoors or from distant window views. But here is an example of how precision placement is crucial in a successful marriage of interior to exterior. At this window, it's hard to tell what is inside from what is outside . . . but then that is the ultimate goal. This technique must be carefully employed, however, because in areas with persistent wind, or where the fountain is incorrectly chosen, water may splash on the window and cause a continuous problem of spotting and mineral buildup. **OPPOSITE RIGHT** This plan illustrates how narrow and linear this landscape is. It wraps around three sides of the house, encompassing the kitchen patio, lawn play area, corner pool, and narrow adult garden with window fountain. Every inch of ground is utilized to its maximum potential for this large family with active children.

Mediocre to Monumental

No matter how dismal your house may appear at the start, the magic of facade enhancement and creative landscape design can indeed change the character of any home and lot. Clearly the wisdom to know what should remain is at the core of any redesign; we so often spend inordinate amounts of time and money on protecting trees. All of us grew up venerating trees, and environmental consciousness today underscores that reverence—but in the contemporary French profile, the liquidambars would have to be removed to make the space work.

Consider every home a gold mine of undiscovered wealth. While homeowners often see the difficulties of remodeling as intimidating, some of the greater limitations often spawn innovative solutions. So embrace your home and lot no matter how ordinary, and rejoice that the problem-solving challenge you or your designer face will no doubt yield a beautiful, surprising landscape that is perfectly adapted to you and your outdoor lifestyle.

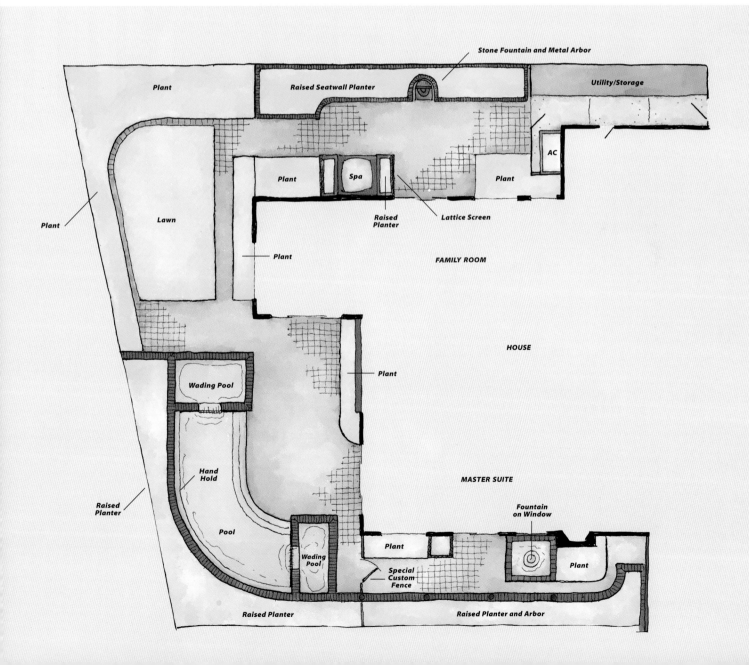

CHAPTER 3

GROWN-UPS ASK FOR A RETREAT FROM THE NOISE AND HUSTLE OF
MODERN STREETS; THEY LIKE TO USE THE GARDEN AS AN EXTRA
ROOM, WHERE, IN SUITABLE WEATHER, MEALS CAN BE TAKEN AND
VISITORS ENTERTAINED.

—H. H. THOMAS, *GARDENING IN TOWNS*, 1936

Condos and Townhouses

Conquering Constraints of Community

TOWNHOUSES ARE THE SMALLEST OF ALL SINGLE-FAMILY DWELLINGS
and are creatures of the city. They have no space between them,
yet remain single-family dwellings. Some have small yards in the
rear that are challenging to make into gardens or outdoor living
spaces; but since this is such precious ground, it deserves special
attention. Condominiums are more often built as small communities. They are generally in clusters sharing parking, open space,
and perhaps a swimming pool. This kind of housing is appealing
because it requires very little care—the common area is main-

tained by the community. Only the rear of the units, which share one or more walls, is available for improvement.

Both townhouses and condominiums are studies in small-scale living. The challenge in this kind of dwelling is not just limited area, it is high-density living in which there is little privacy. You may be able to hear the neighbor's toilet flush and see the tops of their heads next door as they barbecue.

There are three fundamental needs of all condominium and townhouse residents that exist as a factor of urban living:

- *Seclusion* is primary because there may be nothing but neighboring windows looking into the garden. Users should feel a sense of privacy from above and on all sides.
- *Separation* serves to make the dwelling seem as though it is alone in the world, not connected to a dozen other homes. The way separation is achieved must not make the landscape appear walled-in, but instead naturally separated by foliage and artifice.
- *Protection* is always a concern of city living because of high crime levels. The need to create an enclosed space around the building helps make occupants feel more fortified.

In small-space design, it is affordable to use high-quality paving materials. This white paving stone has been applied to both the walking surface and the vertical one on the spa. Discoloration and mineral buildup have occurred on the face of the waterfall.

Breaking the Rules

When you consider spaces in high-density living environments, all bets are off. Designers don't view this kind of work as "how big can it be," but rather "how small can we make it and still ensure functionality." Ultimately, the preconceived dimensions that are accepted as the standards of spatial layout go out the window when the area we are given is tiny. The intent is to push the envelope of convention to see what minimums can be manipulated to suit the landscape.

Walkways and Paving

For example, walkways are generally a minimum of 3 feet (1 meter) wide, considered the optimum balance between comfort of the user and construction costs. The truth is that a person can walk just as comfortably down a path that is 2 feet (60 centimeters) wide, but there will be difficulty negotiating a lawnmower or two-wheeled garden cart without the wheels crushing adjacent plants. Condos and townhouses are generally too small for this kind of equipment anyway, so there is no reason why you can't narrow the walk to 2 feet (60 centimeters) or perhaps 18 inches (45 centimeters) in a pinch.

In a perfect world, we like to have an area at least 100 square feet (10 square meters) to hold a table and four chairs. In fact, it should be larger still for comfortable circulation around the furniture. In many cases, this is a bit too large for a condominium yard, so smaller areas must suffice. The amount of room required for a small café-type table and two chairs is tiny in comparison, so instead of abandoning the idea, we simply change the size of the table.

While lack of space may be difficult to adjust to in terms of layout, it does offer a great deal of opportunity for upgrading materials. When just a few square feet is required, you may choose from far more sophisticated artistic paving materials. Tiles or stonework are suddenly affordable options!

Steps

Any landscape with a change in grade will need steps. Safety is crucial to the design of steps, and there are specific building codes to govern their layout. People become accustomed to steps being a certain height, no matter where you go. These dimensions are based on two planes, the *tread* and the *riser*.

Step treads are where you walk, where your foot meets pavement. The treads should be at least 12 inches (30 centimeters) wide. The only requisite is that all or most of the treads of the step system are made the same width, because users expect that. Sure, they will negotiate variations in situations where a pathway must vary in order to take up the grade logically and beautifully—but in standard steps, continuity ensures safety.

A riser is the vertical face of the step. Codes control this strictly to ensure riser heights range from 6 inches (15 centimeters) to 8.5 inches (21 centimeters) high. If the riser is shorter than this, or if it is overly tall, users not only do not expect it, they may have difficulty negotiating the steps. This is particularly true for older persons or those with disabilities. Again, as with treads, all risers must be uniform, so if you begin with 6 inches (15 centimeters), you finish up with the same. No matter how wide the tread, the riser must be consistent.

Unlike steps indoors, where there is plenty of nighttime illumination, steps outdoors can be very dangerous after dark. Lights are often installed along the edges of narrow garden path steps because they are so small that this light provides all the safety illumination that is needed. But when you have broad steps that are wider than edge lights can cover, there must be lighting overhead to shine down on the steps.

The other option is to install lights into the step riser if it is inappropriate to light from overhead or if there is no overhead structure to support the lights. These step lights not only provide a safer stairway, they add to evening ambience when combined with other lighting systems in the garden. All are manufactured with a hood or louvers to funnel light down onto the adjacent tread gently and specifically in order to avoid conflicts with ambient light.

In a tiny side yard, Nevada moss flagstone set on sand without mortar provides a walking surface without sacrificing the rustic character. Such natural walkways are a bit difficult for high-heeled shoes to negotiate, and so are best left for more casual, out-of-the-way paths.

ABOVE LEFT Even the narrowest gaps between condo units can be made gardenesque by the laying of large Arizona flagstone slabs bordered by babytears. Despite this natural look, this flagstone is quite slip resistant and the slabs are large enough to be easily negotiated in any shoes. Size increases weight, which ensures the slabs remain secure without mortar. **ABOVE RIGHT** You can combine different kinds of high-quality paving to allow a smoother transition from one level to the next for houses situated on hillsides. The key is a smooth connection without footings or excessive mortar showing. **CENTER RIGHT** The stunning beauty of this lovely Indian slate is expressed not only by the great variety of colors, but the geometry of the mortar joints that outline the various sizes. This kind of paving is more expensive, not just because of the material, but the price of skilled stone masons capable of such precise work. **BELOW** Indian slate, just as many other kinds of unusual stone paving units, tends to lose its brilliance rather quickly. This is a benefit in that it blends more naturally with planting, but unfortunate in that it loses its startling, crisp color. Color can, however, be preserved by sealants applied annually, but these will make the surface a bit more slippery in inclement weather.

Frostproof Tile

In order for tile to be resistant to damage from frost, it must be manufactured a certain way. Frost damage occurs when water soaks into the tile, then freezes. This makes the water expand to crack the tile, or sometimes moisture accumulating between the setting bed and the bottom of the tile will pop it right out of place as it freezes.

Porous stone or tile is most subject to frost damage. The test for frostproof tile is to turn the sample upside-down and drop some water on the surface. If it soaks in, the tile is too porous and is not suitable for freezing climates. If it beads up and remains that way indefinitely, it's probably frostproof. Some tile designed for cold weather applications feature extrusions on the back, little ribs or grids that stick out from the body of the tile to help keep it in place.

Among the most porous tiles are those made in Mexico, either terra cotta or the colorful glazed Spanish tiles. Swimming pool companies are great places to hunt for frostproof color tiles; they are used at the waterline, where they are exposed to both excessive moisture and cold.

BELOW LEFT Terra cotta tile is a favorite for Mediterranean-inspired gardens and terraces. The best quality is this even-colored, high-fired, dense type—more expensive but important where extremes of weather demand frostproof ceramics. **CENTER TOP** Mexican terra cotta tiles, called Saltillo pavers, vary in quality relating to the density of the clay and degree of firing. Their color and slight irregularity provide a warmer, more natural feel than the high-fired European types. This step design is simple, with straight face and tread. The risers are decorated with colorful glazed Spanish tiles and bronze lighting fixtures. **CENTER BOTTOM** Steps can feature a cantilevered tread that is best achieved with a poured concrete tread. Here the concrete was tinted a rosy pink and pocked with a salt finish. The thickness of the concrete cantilever leaves a narrow slice of riser visible where accent materials and very thin lighting fixtures are installed. The risers are faced with Italian marble that matches the floors inside, linking the front entry to the overall decorating scheme. **BELOW RIGHT** Bull-nose units of brick or stone feature special edges designed to be canti-levered over steps or pool decks. These steps incorporate an overlarge bullnose cantera stone paver unit that matches the remainder of the site paving. Step risers are faced with Spanish tiles and rectangular louvered lighting fixtures.

Profile: Zen and the Art of Condo Living

Condominium complexes come in all shapes and sizes, laid out in multiple stories or in a sprawling series of connected buildings. In this case, it is a warren of homes and garages arranged around a feeder drive that makes each unit appear like its own individual dwelling. It produced a series of pockets and enclosures defined by the architectural barriers.

For the owners, busy artists dedicated to work, the promises of small-space living are welcome indeed. Yet the home this couple occupied was still far too exposed to the outside world to provide the sensation of a spatial sanctuary amidst urban sprawl. The primary intent was to fully enclose what had been mostly enclosed already, but to finish a secure entry court that would now be accessed by an outer door.

WHATEVER THE UTILITARIAN, AESTHETIC OR OTHER AIMS OF AN ARCHITECT MAY BE, ARCHITECTURE BECOMES MANIFEST BY BARRIERS ENCLOSING SPACE. A PERSON WITHIN THIS DEFINED SPACE IS SUBJECT TO THE SUBCONSCIOUS SPATIAL SENSATION.

—ERNO GOLDFINGER, *THE SENSATION OF SPACE*, 1941

This condominium community did not allow any new fencing inside the development, which made it difficult for the owners to achieve the sense of privacy desired. Originally, they had proposed a Chinese moon door; then, due to cost overruns, sought out a salvage door, but could find nothing suitable. Ultimately, they hired an artist to design the current door and then took the plans to the association in an application for a variance. It was finally granted, and the door was fabricated. This illustrates one important point about condominium complex variances—if you apply, your proposition had better be good and in keeping with the overall architectural character. If it's not coordinated, there's little chance of an official dispensation.

Once the fence and doorway were in place, the primary challenge of the site was posed by the entry walkway, which accessed the garage door at least 30 inches (75 centimeters) below the front door to the house. Even worse, only 10 or 15 feet (3 or 5 meters) was available in which to take up the grade. The choice for solving such a tight grade peccadillo was wood deck, because this would not require such extensive footings as masonry work. To maximize the amount of usable space at the ultimate finish-floor elevation, the grade change had to be achieved up front without appearing cramped or forced.

While the front entry court garden is not large by any means, the rear yard is truly minuscule in comparison. Windows opening onto this narrow strip of precious real estate and the fence beyond offered nothing to enhance the experience from the interior. Yet during very hot summer days, this eastern exposure is a welcome respite, despite the proximity of neighbors.

The key was to somehow finagle a living space out of what was clearly a transient experience. To bring it into conjunction with the living room, the paving was pushed up tight against the building. This left only a few spare inches (or centimeters) of planting along the opposite fence if there was to be room for just

Despite the presence of beautiful double doors in line with this new outer entry, the actual front door is in the niche to the left. To emphasize this without obstructing the view, the decking was laid on a diagonal to point the guests in the direction they should go. The small, preexisting planter at left was refaced with cantera tile in a color that blended well with the deck and siding color. The dwarf Japanese black pine (*Pinus thunbergii*) is the first glimpse of a recurring theme in this garden, the use of bonsai more as decorative ornament than the true living plant it is. Beyond the door at right is the garage's pedestrian entry.

two comfortable chairs. Above all, the need to block out neighbors was critical, for to find the separate serenity that artists need and love, there had to be a tall barrier that would not infringe upon the community architectural standards or the neighbors' sensibilities!

What this experience in small-scale living teaches us is that it is indeed the structures, the architectural barriers, that define space. The challenge is to turn that space into a varied experience. This means a balancing act between visibility from indoor rooms, usability of outdoor rooms, and a compartmentalization very much like the floor plan of a house. It is also a study in mitigation: the breaking up of long, narrow spaces by creative paving orientation. It is the funneling of our attention in the direction desired. It is the shrouding of a building in vines to make it more like the edge of an impenetrable forest than a place where our cars reside beyond a very thin wall.

Harmony is expressed, as it is in Eastern consciousness, by the continuity of materials and colors so that all is of equal value, of equal beauty. Although the front court is light and bright and the rear soft and moody, they are connected by a house where people live. This gives them the option of whether to meet the sun or hide from it outdoors at any time of day. Then, while residing in the room of their contentment, they may appreciate the natural beauty, the art created by their own hands, and the centuries-old traditions of bamboo, Buddha, and bonsai.

NEAR RIGHT The use of modular decking units allowed maximum flexibility in terms of overlapping steps to meet grade of house to garage. The dynamics of the block geometry combined with diagonal planking produced remarkable drama in just a few square feet. The dark tile paving at right extends to the outer door. The paving to the left extends to the garage—its wall is partially visible. The use of groundcover mondo grass (*Ophiopogon japonicus*) grants these very crucial edges the rigid control of Asian gardens. Kaffir lilies (*Clivia miniata*), which blossom in *Amaryllis*-like bright orange in spring, and Japanese maple (*Acer japonica*), which will turn scarlet in autumn, provide nearly year-round color and variety. A single well-chosen and well-placed stone is in perfect harmony with such a small pocket planting. **BELOW NEAR RIGHT** As you step up to the main level of the decking, the garden reveals itself, sequestered behind the garage, which is so shrouded in vines it nearly disappears. Only the artist's sculpture reminds us it is there, suspended from an outrigger securely fastened into the wall. On the deck there is room for a small grouping of teak furniture finished in the same hues as the surrounding woodwork. Beyond is the koi pond, a magical natural spring that seems to be a remnant of some primitive grotto built aeons before the surrounding development. That is just the intent—a success, as it was created long after. **TOP CENTER RIGHT** Only by looking back from the koi pond can you see the actual front door. It reveals the remarkable simplicity of the site and how the decking is integrated into the pond feature. The cantilevered effect gives the illusion that the water is one with the living space, not a separate entity existing adjacent to the living space. This sense of integration is essential in small spaces, for the slightest failure to attend to transitions will cause flaws to stand out starkly, ruining the entire effect. **TOP FAR RIGHT** The color palette of the garden, something that is crucial to an artist, must be in complete harmony. While planters are filled with traditional plants, this glazed ceramic pot and its exotic contents are chosen to complement the coral red door panels, reminiscent of early California modern architecture on a diminutive scale. **BELOW FAR RIGHT** The art of koi pond creation and the use of natural stone in such a composition is truly the work of masters. Above all, there is no concrete or mortar visible. This is critical because at this scale, even a small oversight will stand out starkly. The stones are placed around the edge so that they either cantilever over the water or sit partway submerged—just as they would in a natural setting. The planting is also illustrative of what is appropriate for a shaded ferny spring, with California maidenhair fern (*Adiantum jordanii*) in the foreground and its cousin, five-finger fern (*Adiantum peltatum*), up in a rock niche. Larger arching mother ferns (*Asplenium bulbiferum*) are clustered at water's edge, with all shaded by pink flowering dogwoods (*Cornus florida* 'Rubra').

RIGHT The virtual bowling alley of a yard flanked by multistory buildings on both sides proved to be a challenge. The walkway could have indeed been a bowling alley had it not been altered wherever possible to break up the long, narrow line. On the left is a small lily pond that receives just enough sunlight for these aquatic plants to grow. A very narrow slot on the right, barely a foot (30 centimeters) wide, is devoted to bamboo, perhaps the only plant capable of reaching such height and beauty in such a thin space. **BELOW RIGHT** The only exterior access to the rear yard is through the back gate, which could not be altered due to the community regulations. All the paving had to be worked so it met the gate while preserving the privacy of these rear windows. **BELOW LEFT** Not all bamboo is the same. This species of black bamboo (*Phyllostachys nigra*) is among the most beautiful of all—as the canes age, they turn a rich ebony color. The key to making the most of it is to prune shoots and leaves so that the stand remains as narrow and clean as possible. If left to grow naturally, the canes would be shrouded in foliage and never properly appreciated.

ABOVE The crowning gem of the rear yard is a picture-perfect sitting area for two right off the sliding glass doors to the living room. In a space that most would consider too small to work with, Michael has created a virtual microcosm of the Asian expression with two sides backing up to a nondescript fence, the third to a sliding glass door, and the last to a bowling-alley rear yard. To tone down the oppressive fences, they are broken up by bamboo panels that support purple clematis (*Clematis Jackmanii*) and other lacy foliage vines. Where there is no room for trees, there is instead a forest of bonsai that may be tended as one takes tea with the Buddha as both interior and exterior harmony are achieved after a hectic day in the world. **LEFT** Just behind the unique modern bird feeder, a miniature spotlight is mounted on the vine-covered wall. It is so small as to be easily overlooked, but it illuminates the koi pond waterfall on the far side of this garden. The ability of these new high-tech outdoor lighting systems to control the nighttime experience is unmatched by older unattractive fixtures.

Atriums Ad Infinitum

We inherit the word *atrium* from the Romans, who used it to describe the open courtyard around which their traditional rooms were arranged. It was indeed a light-giving place, and today its legacy is any outdoor space incorporated into a building.

Atriums became a popular means of making high-density housing seem open and gardenesque within the original building footprint. Their use was common in condominiums and even apartments. Townhouses of New Orleans's French Quarter often included such places in an attempt to mitigate the stifling heat and humidity before modern refrigeration.

Today, atriums are magical places that have one foot indoors and the other outdoors, and are sufficiently sheltered so that often the limitations of cold hardiness in plants may be challenged. It is usually highly visible from key rooms of the house, and so the small-space garden maker delights in the opportunity to bring the best of the landscape into this tiny environment.

Among the most difficult conditions of the atrium is the soil. Surrounded by concrete or masonry footings on three or more sides, there may be virtually no drainage, the soil contaminated by lime leaching out of the concrete into this tiny spot of earth. Underground utilities, basements, bedrock, and dozens of other constraints make atrium work in natural soil difficult, often impossible.

Simple solutions for atriums are to pave or surface the entire area to improve access and offer a well-drained surface for artistic container gardens. Wood decks, concrete slabs, and various types of masonry paver tiles are all suitable, and since these areas are tiny, high-priced options are made quite affordable.

Atriums are also terrific places for water features because the sounds bounce off walls to magnify the ambience. When windows and doors are thrown open to atrium water features, there is a dramatic change in the character of the room.

Walls are crucial to the success of atrium treatments. They provide a great surface for suspending practically anything that can be hung safely. These include wall fountains of bronze or iron, and art pieces both new and antique. Best of all is the opportunity to hang pots and baskets both from the overheads and as sconces, multiplying the amount of verdant foliage and brilliant flowers far and above what can be grouped exclusively on the ground plain.

In a tiny atrium barely 25 square feet (8 square meters), a world of interest can be created by a careful hand. An antique pot has been filled with water to create a mirror-like surface. On the wall is a reproduction of an ancient stone panel made of light-weight fiberglass for easy anchoring. The pygmy date palm, *Phoenix robellini*, is treasured for its small stature. Bronze exotic bromeliads combine with ferns and river cobbles to create a superbly crafted still life.

ABOVE A dining room, once open to the neighbor's house windows, was enclosed into a sliver of a private atrium with an exotic effect that evokes the South Pacific. Michael custom-designed this water-wall with natural flagstone veneer. The adjacent walls are covered with bamboo screens integrated with potted golden bamboo (*Phyllostachys aurea*). **LEFT** The water feature dynamics are revealed here. Water spills out of a trough along the top of this wall to cascade down the flagstone face, splashing over small shelves of stone to create the desired sound effect. Under the black pebbles at the bottom is a collection basin that gathers and recirculates the water invisibly. Potted freesias, bamboo, and maidenhair ferns complete the spare yet deliberate planting scheme.

Profile: Old World Elegance

The owner of this garden condominium unit had both entry court and rear yard to work with, and a grossly incompetent landscaper had failed to get beyond planting a few shrubby magnolias. The owner was well off financially and quite willing to pay for quality landscape, but thousands of dollars and six months later the garden was nothing but old broken concrete, debris piles, and weeds.

Michael calls them the walking wounded: homeowners suffering from havoc caused by incompetent landscapers. By the time he comes on the scene, they're really gun-shy. It takes him awhile to gain their confidence, but once they get started, the first order of business is undoing what should never have been done in the first place.

The interior scheme, with snow-white carpeting and gilded furniture, had a level of decorating perfection that contrasted starkly with the wreckage outside the windows. The shades were perpetually drawn against the ugly mess of a yard, making the already small dwelling seem like a city apartment.

IF YOU ACCEPT ART, IT MUST BE PART OF YOUR DAILY LIVES, AND THE DAILY LIFE OF EVERY MAN. IT WILL BE WITH US WHEREVER WE GO, IN THE ANCIENT CITY FULL OF TRADITIONS OF PAST TIME, IN THE NEWLY CLEARED FARM IN AMERICA. . . .

—WILLIAM MORRIS, *THE LESSER ARTS*, 1882

Michael's first instinct was to tear out just about everything and start over, because there was little worth the effort of salvage. Concrete exposed aggregate slabs were cracked by tree roots and could not be veneered because they were too thin to start. Overlaying such low-quality concrete work is dangerous because there will almost certainly be further movement.

The overall concept of this garden was based on the owner's love of antiques, and such old museum pieces were part of the interior decor. These objects of art and artifacts would be used throughout the garden to provide timeless sophistication and interest beyond what was achieved with plants. Unlike most landscapes, this one would feature true antiques many centuries old from Africa and the Middle East. The overriding themes would be rooted in classical civilizations along with many primitive pieces that exhibited the timeless patina of age.

The result was a dramatic makeover of a below-average condominium. The front entry, deeply recessed into the building and accessed by a narrow walk through an enclosed courtyard, was indeed tiny. Therefore, everything had to be perfect to the last detail—beginning with the old concrete walk, which was broken up, removed, and replaced with a new walkway of light cantera tile built over a slab. The narrow planters around the edges were planted to create the greatest amount of diversity and still retain an integrated scheme.

The water feature in this diminutive space had to be small and controlled. It was custom-created using a large pot with an antique glaze and a fish spout to provide a very controlled, focused stream of water. Antique pots, benches, and other wall decorations were used for the recessed entry, which was as narrow as an interior hallway.

The entry garden features a young Mediterranean fan palm (*Chamerops humilis*), which is one of the most versatile and frost hardy of the small bedding scale palms. This palm is most often treated like a shrub rather than a tree. It is very slow-growing and tends to develop multiple trunks over many decades, which makes mature specimens popular nightlighting subjects. It is hardy to cold snaps as low as 6 degrees Fahrenheit (−14 degrees Celsius), but will not survive prolonged cold weather.

The rear yard of the condo, which was viewed from the living room and dining room through large glass doors, was recreated with the same character as the front garden. All original concrete was removed and replaced with the cantera tile over slab. A raised seatwall planter was constructed along the back fence to break up the continuous barrier and provide the environment for a water feature.

It's important to know that this condominium is located where summers are long and hot. Outdoor living is popular, but only where there is sufficient shade; and due to pronounced glare, planting must be composed of an abundance of soothing green foliage in order to appear refreshing on the hottest days. This, more than the need for vibrant color, makes the rear yard scheme so attractive both indoors and out.

The front gate to the enclosed entry courtyard is transparent, giving visitors a full view of this postage-stamp garden. Under the window is a partially buried ceramic oil jar, the first of many antique pieces used throughout the landscape.

ABOVE LEFT The partially buried jar is a hallmark technique of Michael's work. An olive oil urn, imported from Crete, is gently nestled in delphiniums and blooming impatiens. **ABOVE RIGHT** From the front door alcove, the fountain becomes the visual focal point. Simple and self-contained, it is composed of an antique pot from Thailand and a bronze fish spout, grounded by river cobbles and moss rocks around the base. Surrounding plants include a sago palm (*Cycas revoluta*) on the right and a Mediterranean fan palm (*Chamerops humilis*) on the left. Large-leaf dwarf southern magnolias frame the view.

There were some existing trees closer up to the building that were left for shade, but the new paving was worked around them due to surface rooting that cracked the original paving. This illustrates one of the caveats of landscape remodeling where trees exist. If they tend to be surface-rooted or are made that way due to previous watering methods, the problem will not go away. You cannot raise soil up around the trunk without killing the tree. Cutting the roots doesn't help either, and it may risk the tree's health.

As a result, the paving in this courtyard is, above all, responsive to constraints of the tree roots. Some of the living space had to be sacrificed to the trees, so the planting areas on the opposite side had to be pushed back to a minimum. These narrow areas would be planted in soft plants, mostly perennials, and espaliered

woody specimens that could be kept up flat against the fence and never threaten the paving with roots.

Though this entire project measured just a few hundred square feet, it fulfilled the owner's every wish. The entry invites us in and promises surprises around every corner. The rear view, now from the living room, is both simple and exotic. The rear patio is large enough for roomy outdoor dining, with attractive, soothing plants at every turn. It is a landscape rooted in the art of classical Mediterranean civilization, exhibiting the simple sophistication of both the owner and the interior.

As the Victorian designer William Morris said, "If you accept art, it must be part of your daily life." This landscape is full of relics of ancient cities amidst the landscape of America, condensed into a most perfect condo garden.

The new view from the living room is now focused on the far raised planter with its lovely birdbath fountain custom-carved in Mexico from cantera stone. It matches the veneer on the wall and the paving, providing a fully integrated space large enough for comfortable outdoor dining.

The planter doubles as extra seating due to the comfortable bull-nose cap units on top. The edges of seatwall planters are rough on nylon hose or knit clothing if the cap units are not smooth and rounded. Two levels allow seating, and the upper is ideal for setting a plate or drink while socializing. Large ferns and rhododendrons fill the planter and thrive in the shady, moist environment.

LEFT The fountain was custom-designed by Michael and carved in Mexico out of cantera stone. The round medallion accent pieces are old bronze hardware from Spanish colonial doors. They bear the verdigris patina, and over time the cantera will begin to discolor with moss and algae, making the contrast between new and old less marked. **BELOW LEFT** This view from just outside the living room doors looks back to the more functional door from the kitchen–dining area on the far right. This is the narrowest part of the garden, illustrating how tight the dimensions of the planting strip at the fence really are. In the foreground is an example of how the existing trees were accommodated. The trunk at left is shrouded in needlepoint ivy, and an old water jar was used to add interest to the planting there, which was limited because surface roots made it nearly impossible to plant anything there. Only dwarf palms and ferns had rootballs soft enough to grow here. **BELOW RIGHT** The wall of the neighboring unit is two stories with no relief. This very large bas relief of Mercury's wing is a reproduction of an old Roman work. It is manufactured in lightweight fiberglass and is a very well-done example of quality reproduction. The dimensions are over 2 by 3 feet (60 by 90 centimeters) in size, and a true stone or ceramic piece would be impossibly heavy. The fiberglass makes this detail suitable for any application with no need for structural reinforcement.

Palms and Cycads

There is often confusion between palms and cycads—probably because our most common cycad is commonly called *sago palm*, which is misleading. Cycads are a group of living fossil plants that have not changed in millions of years. They are virtually evolutionary dead ends and are actually more closely related to pine trees than anything else, because cycads reproduce by cones. Cycads as a rule are not very frost hardy, and so are grown in pots in colder climates in order that they may be moved indoors for the winter.

Palms are a huge group that reproduce very differently than cycads. Only the shape and leaf type make cycads similar to palms. Since plants are classified by their reproductive structures, such as flowers and fruit, and not by their appearance, cycads and palms are very different. There is a group of palms commonly used in small-scale landscapes, be they atriums or courtyards. Some are very frost hardy, while others are nearly tropical. These are the small palms most often used in flowerbed conditions, and are ideal for landscapes short on space.

Botanical Name	Common Name	Hardiness (Degrees F = C)
Chamerops humilis	Mediterranean fan palm	6°F (−14°C)
Phoenix reclinata	Senegal date palm	20°F (−7°C)
Phoenix robellini	Pygmy date palm	32°F (0°C)
Trachycarpus fortunei	Windmill palm	5°F (−21°C)

Palm trees in general are more frost hardy as adults than as juveniles. Those with fat trunks tend to stand up to cold better than those with thinner trunks. This is due to the fact that palms have no cambium layer, but are more like grasses, with their trunks composed of bundles of fleshy water-carrying tubes. Each time a younger palm is exposed to frost, some of the outer tubes freeze and die. Over many frosts there can develop a thick layer of dead tubes that act very much like a blanket to insulate the inner living tubes from freezing.

Therefore, palms that survive cold through adolescence tend to be very hardy adults. Palms that have thin trunks may end up sacrificing too many tubes to frost and, as a result, lose vigor as their vital tubes dwindle to critical numbers. The small windmill palm is extremely hardy as palms go, despite its very thin trunk, compared to the Mediterranean fan palm. The windmill palm produces an outer blanket of fibers around the petioles of the leaves, and this adds frost protection without sacrificing vital tissues.

Planting the Narrows

The art of planting narrow spaces is the base of most urban garden concepts. Where every inch is crucial and there is a disproportionate ratio of hardscape to planting, the forcing of small plants into strips of earth is the only way many areas will ever see green.

Landscapers resist creating planting areas less than 3 feet (1 meter) wide. This is not altogether in the client's best interest, but that of expediency and standards. Narrower planters are more difficult to adapt to irrigation because there are difficulties in tight spaces where pipes interfere with the ability to plant a sizable rootball. Ultimately, the adjustment proves to be smaller container plant material and creative sprinkler piping diagrams. The sprinkler heads may require bubblers that flood and do not spot windows, or soaker tubing that sweats water over a long line instead of at individual points. Microspray and drip systems have proved highly adapted to these conditions, but are somewhat vulnerable to severe, cold winters.

The position of strips must respond in part to what can be viewed from the interior, and the view from most standard windows is that of the far side of the space. For sliding glass doors or where the plate glass begins at floor level, the need is for planting immediately in front of the window. Often, this is simply a 1-foot- (30-centimeter-)wide ribbon where tiny plants grow to cover up the ugly intersection of horizontal and vertical planes. The term *needlepoint gardening* has often been applied to just such a condition. The plants used might include thrift (*Armeria meritima*), maidenhair fern, crocus bulbs, sedum, violets, and babytears.

When considering plants for townhouse and condominium landscapes, careful attention must be paid to both overall size and rooting characteristics. The greatest source of conflict among neighbors, particularly in the close quarters of city yards and condominium complexes, is the result of roots and branches extending beyond the fence line. Improper plants cause increased maintenance and uncontrolled spreading, both underground and overhead.

These are examples of the most common points of contention among neighbors in high-density complexes:

- Roots traveling under fences force neighbors to hack through them to make holes for their own plants.
- Roots cause cracking of paving in neighbor's yard or common areas.
- Spreading shrubs place horizontal stress on fences and cause them to lean.
- Uncontrolled vines and groundcovers spread to invade planting and structures.
- Tree limbs overhanging next door cause litter and reduce sunlight.

Avoid Large, Woody Shrubs

Woody shrubs are the most frequent offenders in every landscape situation. Many common landscape shrubs reach 10 or 12 feet (3 or 4 meters) tall and nearly as wide at maturity, yet time after time they are planted under eaves in planters just 3 or 4 feet (1 meter) wide. As a result, routine shearing becomes unavoidable, because without it the adjacent walkway would become overwhelmed and impassable. Plant such a shrub in a small-scale landscape, and you are assured loads of trouble and maintenance in the very near future.

Avoid Fast-Growing or Large Trees

Avoid fast-growing trees, which are the temptation of all impatient gardeners. The time needed to see a quality tree reach maturity is often beyond the tolerance of some, and so they fall for the fast-growth lure over that of beauty or suitability. Among the major offenders are willows, acacia, fruitless mulberry, eucalyptus, and locust. The old saying "Choose the right plant for the right place" is evidenced here. Fast-growing trees have proved to be short-lived, disease prone, weak limbed, and invasively rooted.

Small trees for small landscapes include:

- Japanese maple (*Acer japonicum*)
- Pink flowering dogwood (*Cornus florida 'Rubra'*)
- Crepe myrtle (*Lagerstroemia indica*)
- Australian tea tree (*Leptospermum lavaegatum*)
- Mayten tree (*Maytenus boaria*)

Weatherproof works of art can be used to dress up bare walls without sacrificing any living space. This sheet-metal tree with roots is treated with chemicals to produce the blue-green verdigris finish, which will look better and better over time.

Choose Herbaceous Plants That Are Naturally Small

Herbaceous plants lack woody stems, and most die down for the winter. They reach a limited size, and, due to their soft parts, they do not exert pressure on fences or other plants nearby. The most popular for sunny, small gardens are perennials; but in the shade, ferns and hostas are most common.

Choose Dwarf Shrubs

Many larger shrubs have younger brothers called dwarfs. These may occur naturally, such as is the case with Oregon grape (*Mahonia aquifolium*), which has a smaller relative called *Mahonia aquifolium 'compacta.'* Other plants were developed through breeding or grafting to be naturally dwarf. The common mock orange (*Pittosporum tobira*) has a newer variety that's very small called *Pittosporum tobira 'Wheeler's Dwarf.'* Always seek out the dwarf forms of familiar shrubs to find the most appropriate plants for small gardens.

Use Only Well-Behaved Vines and Groundcovers

Many of our most common landscape vines are huge plants even before they reach maturity. Fast growth and the ability to weave themselves make them excellent shade arbor plants, but a nemesis in small spaces. Once you plant a fast vine or groundcover, if not perpetually controlled and cut back, it will literally take over your yard and the neighbor's. English ivy is a good example of what happens when you let such an enormous plant climb up a tree—vine beats tree every time. Therefore, choose vines that are slow-growing, or very lacy like clematis.

Explore vines that are slow and controllable.

- *Clematis* hybrids
- Lavender trumpet vine (*Clytostoma callistigioides*)
- Creeping fig (*Ficus pumula*)
- Morning glory (*Ipomoea tricolor*)
- Chinese jasmine (*Jasminum polyanthum*)

Ignore vines that are too large or too fast-growing.

- Trumpet creeper (*Campsis radicans*)
- English ivy (*Hedera helix*)
- Honeysuckle (*Lonicera japonica*)
- Wisteria (*Wisteria sinensis*)

Patio Trees: It's All About Training

Topiary trees aren't really trees—they're shrubs trained into tree shapes. Actually, it's more like a lollipop shape, with a straight stem topped by a perfect ball of foliage. This neat shape can be kept to a consistent size, ensuring that it never outgrows its space. This miniature technique has hit the commercial growers market, and they have produced the perfect product for small-scale landscapes: they're called *patio trees*. The plants they use aren't trees, but shrubs trained from a very early age to this form, which makes them a bit more expensive to buy as they are sold in 5-gallon (19-liter) containers.

Patio trees are often grown in large ornamental pots on decks or patios, in atriums or courtyards. These plants can also be used outdoors permanently if your climate is such that they are sufficiently hardy, but most plants grown this way are evergreen and somewhat tender. Designers like them because of a uniformity of growth, which means that they are standardized, and most of those sold are about the same age and size. It's common to choose two matched patio trees to flank doorways, gates, or entry planters. You'll see a number of them used in a row to define edges or create outdoor partitions for enclosure.

Some patio trees flower, while others are more static and ask only for an occasional shaping with electric clippers. They are quite exposed, however, and may not be suited for very cold climates unless you bring them indoors for winter, which is why they are often planted in pots. You'll find their formality quite compatible with most pots, be they classical, glazed, or antiqued.

Types of Patio Trees Available

Some of these plants can be found in as many as a dozen different varieties.

Tender Plants

Abutilon hybridum	*Eugenia myrtifolia*
Azalea southern indica	*Gardenia jasminoides*
Bougainvillea	*Hibiscus rosa-sinensis*
Camellia japonica	*Lantana*
Citrus pardisi	*Nerium oleander*
Citrus reticulata	*Citrus sinensis*

Hardy and Half-Hardy Plants

Chamaecyparis obtusa	*Lagerstroemia indica*
Cotoneaster dammeri	*Ligustrum texanum*
Euonymus kiautschovica	*Picea abies*
Ilex aquifolium	*Puncia granatum*
Juniperus chinensis	*Pyracantha angustifolia*
Juniperus horizontalis	*Raphiolepis indica*
Juniperus scopulorum	

Afterthoughts on High-Density Living

There are many reasons why small residential communities are so attractive, from better security to less home maintenance. But no matter how much you travel or how many hours you spend at the office, this place is still your home. It is essentially all the elements of a single-family house with front and back yard condensed into a microcosm, a vestige of this tradition. Therefore, to complete the holistic home environment, there must be a tiny outdoor space where we can go out to feel the sun on our face, the soft breezes of late summer, or the bite of winter cold amidst fallen snow. And while there, imagine it in its greatest glory without giving a second thought to who will mow the lawn.

CHAPTER 4

THE EXTERIOR APPOINTMENTS OF [A MAN'S] HOME STAND FOR WHAT HE HIMSELF IS. IF THESE BE CHEAP AND TAWDRY HE IS JUDGED TO HIS PREJUDICE, BUT IF THE ARRANGEMENT IS ORDERLY AND ARTISTIC, HE IS CREDITED ACCORDINGLY.

—ROBERT B. CRIDLAND,

PRACTICAL LANDSCAPE GARDENING, 1916

Reclaim Your Lost Front Yard

It's Yours . . . Why Give It to the Street?

CIVIC PRIDE WAS A GREAT THEME OF THE NINETEENTH CENTURY, A time when all things changed in America. No longer were great homes the exclusive realm of the very rich. The common working class found that they could now afford a house in the city or suburbs that gave their family both comfort and status. In this vein the early subdivisions were formed, the lot and block expanses of wood frame houses on individual lots.

Like the model of rich tycoons, small lots also attempted sweeping walkways, arboretums of trees, and exotic-looking plants in the front gardens. These landscapes became a barometer of the owner's taste and status. Far more time and energy was spent maintaining this statement than enjoying it.

As the twentieth century emerged, the front gardens lost much of their highly ornamented qualities. They were often little more than broad lawns with a few trees. As land values increased, the position of new homes changed. They were moved progressively farther back on the lot to benefit community spaciousness, which left even less living space in the rear. City planners mandated rigid setbacks from curb to house. This ensured wide streets, parkways for boulevard trees, and broad lawns, which all combined to create a very broad cross section that looked great on paper.

The trouble was that Americans were changing the way they used their lots. The postwar nuclear family lost much of its interest in impressing the neighborhood with wasted space. Suddenly there was a demand for patios and lawns for outdoor living and children.

In the postwar building boom, there arose a clash between old-fashioned city planners and builders who were throwing up subdivisions as fast as the new families could buy them. No one wanted a big front yard anymore, and gradually the houses moved forward to the center of the lot. Yet the old requirements of building codes limited the homeowner and builder as to how close they could actually come to the street. It also limited what permanent alterations and construction could occur between the building and the curb.

Building Code Limits to Front Yard Reclamation and Ways to Get Around Them

Understanding your front yard potential is based upon the kind of neighborhood you live in. Some will enforce more standard building codes, while others are quite picky. In concept, the codes are designed to protect our property values, not to limit our use of them. Yes, there is always someone who paints her house purple or chartreuse, and codes are written to reduce the impact of these less-than-ideal artistic expressions on neighborhood property values.

THERE IS ALWAYS SOMEONE ON THE BLOCK WHO PAINTS HIS HOUSE PURPLE. IT IS PART OF HUMAN NATURE, THE ASSERTION OF INDIVIDUALITY AMIDST WIDESPREAD UNIFORMITY.

—MURPHY'S LAW

The most basic front yard codes relate to setback. This is usually the distance from the back of the curb, or back of the sidewalk, to the closest corner of the house. In a traditional tract house, the garage projects outward from the body of the house. The face of the garage is the limit line. You can't build any fence or freestanding walls any taller than 30 inches (75 centimeters) or 3 feet (90 centimeters) between the face of the garage and the street. This allows for the white picket fence, as long as no part of it exceeds 3 feet (90 centimeters).

A Double Wall Solution

Michael Glassman encountered front yard code limitations in an old subdivision where the homeowner wished to have a private front courtyard on the east side of

Perhaps it is due to poverty, and the ensuing crime's security demands. But whatever the reason, you will rarely see a house in the middle-class neighborhoods of Mexico City. Here we find a complete reversal of the exaggerated sense of American civic pride. Mexican homes are bound by walls and iron fences that line the backs of the sidewalks. The houses themselves and their driveways are inaccessible from the street except through gates. This is true even on very modestly sized lots.

As a child, I lived with my family in one of these modest, walled homes in the suburb of Lomas. We spent as much time in the front yard as we did in the rear, if not more. This front utilization allowed us two separate exposures rather than one, and doubled the outdoor living space. Plus, we kids could play there protected from strangers. We were never bothered by solicitors or unwelcome visitors; the bell was down at the gate, and we could see who was there through the kitchen window.

What we learn from Mexico City is that our priorities may be out of line when it comes to front yards. The homeowner has a right to use every inch of his or her precious land, particularly where property prices have skyrocketed. The impact of this on neighborhood beauty is not nearly as detrimental as you might think, and with the rise of gang activity, the older building codes may be sorely out of date. After all, most Beverly Hills homes are hidden behind impenetrable walls of shrubbery, which is only possible because these residences are so large.

her house, which faced the street. It was the only outdoor exposure that received morning sun. In this case, her garage was set farther back than the front of the house, dictating that no barrier could exceed the 3-foot (90-centimeter) height limit dictated by the code. The key to the solution was in knowing that the code dictated that nothing *constructed* could exceed the height limit—which did not include plants.

Michael's creative solution involved extending the height of the walled enclosure with plants. He could have used nothing but plants for the same end, but it would take years for them to achieve a tall, hedgelike screening effect. But if they were placed in a raised planter, it would automatically add 3 feet (90 centimeters) to their overall height at the outset.

The design pushed the code to the highest wall possible (3 feet or 90 centimeters), and a second wall paralleled it to create a 3-foot- (90-centimeter-)deep raised planter over the entire length. When backfilled, this brought the soil level to the top of the walls, and then an assortment of shrubs and small trees were planted densely enough for screening. The result was an instant enclosure that was opaque on the bottom half and translucent on the upper half to allow light and air movement without sacrificing privacy or violating codes. Over time, the owner would be able to control the density of the planting, as well as its overall height, to meet her personal preference.

The plants chosen to raise the privacy level above that of the walls had to be tolerant of shade and the eventual acidity caused by the influence of the existing cedar tree. Azaleas, camellias, and ferns are all acid-loving plants. They were also chosen by Michael right at the nursery as specimens, which in the trade means they are abnormally large and sold in 15-gallon (57-liter) containers or the equal in balled and burlapped stock. This provided the homeowner with the maximum

ABOVE LEFT This beautiful old 1920s home had the typical Italianate facade that presents challenges similar to those faced in many urban homes and row houses with tiny front yards. The low walls shown here are made more attractive by a contrasting extruded cap and custom-built arched iron double gates. Michael also had the concrete walk widened and resurfaced with tile to add a more grand sense of entry. Note the large deodar cedar to the left, the reason why the courtyard is smaller on one side. **ABOVE RIGHT** This view from the inside of the courtyard shows the walls, still as free of stains and the effects of water seepage as the day they were completed. They hold a lovely New Zealand tree fern (*Dicksonia antarctica*) that picks up the morning sun and diffuses it into soft lime-colored hues. Potted plants are arranged around the toe of the wall to make the furniture appear more nestled into the landscape. The beautiful contrasting cap is much more visible here at close range.

amount of privacy possible from the very beginning. Over time, the plants have spread out, achieving their individual characters and increasing the overall sense of seclusion.

Remodel for Second Entry Solution

Many people separate garden remodeling from house remodeling, but the really brilliant solutions come from a little bit of both. Yet another house that confronted Michael faced east. The front wall, entry door, and kitchen windows all opened onto the same wall. The exterior finish material of the house was accented by some unique scored concrete block.

The solution was to create a second entry portico, a feature that shows up in many of Michael's projects. The new entry extended out from the face of the house and contained a doorway itself. There was a continuous roof line from the new wall to the front entry door. This extruded masonry facade pushed the legal front edge of the house out well over 10 feet (3 meters).

This allowed a new horizontal screen fence that ran all the way across the front of the building and then turned back again at a second masonry gateway. This changed the dynamics of the kitchen, and a simple 6-foot- (2-meter-)wide window was quickly made into a sliding door. Now the breakfast nook opens onto a sunny morning courtyard with complete privacy.

LEFT The scored masonry block already existing on the house is shown at left. This is part of the new extension, attached to the entry feature and the outer door. The visitor passes through the court-yard to the old front door and into the house itself. The white lattice fence now separates the courtyard from the street just a few yards beyond. It allows air and light to pass through and keeps the courtyard fresh and comfortable, even in the heat of summer. **CENTER** This courtyard doesn't have a square inch of living space to spare for planting. Those planters at the foot of the fence are only 18 inches (45 centi-meters) wide, just enough for fragrant jasmine vines (*Jasminum polyanthum*), which have traveled up and over the top. A second vertical gardening tech-nique is used here—the hanging moss baskets suspended from outrigger brackets. The rest of the planting is composed of rich green foliage plants. Large-leaf English laurel (*Prunus laurocerasus*) combines with dainty maidenhair fern (*Adiantum jordanii*), azaleas, Japanese maple (*Acer japonica*), and the fine babytears groundcover (*Soleirolia soleirolii*), which absorb light and soften the glare of the white fence and masonry. Paving is a small 8-inch (20-centimeter) terra cotta paver. **BELOW LEFT** This view shows the linear layout of the front court-yard. To the right and back is a glimpse of the new front door under the extended roof line. **BELOW RIGHT** The second opening on the left is the new sliding door to the kitchen. To the rear is a new wall completing the far end of the courtyard with concrete block bearing patterns, ventilation holes, and motifs typical of this 1960s architecture.

Fin Wall Solution

Often the homeowner wishes to have a much better view out the front window than just passing cars and lawn. The ability to make a front courtyard partition part of the house allows you to exceed even the maximum code height limits for fences and walls, which is usually 6 feet (2 meters). Attachment actually changes how the wall is viewed by building departments because it is now house in terms of the law.

THE ESSENTIAL THING OF BOTH ROOM AND
SQUARE IS THE QUALITY OF ENCLOSED SPACE.
—CAMILLO SITTE, *THE ART OF BUILDING CITIES*, 1945

In another example of Michael's problem-solving ability, this building connection was carried to its limit. The home fronted on a cul-de-sac, with a pie-shaped lot leaving barely enough front yard for a tiny lawn and some bushes. The very large front window opened from a lovely white and gilded living room, its luxury not at all enhanced by sidewalks and a huge black asphalt turnaround in the view. Taking the white slump block material from the house entry, he extended a wall out into a perfect geometric semicircle that disappeared into a narrow side yard on the opposite edge.

The key is that the wall intersected the house only on one side, which fulfilled the criteria. What makes it awesome is that the height of the wall is 10 feet (3 meters)! This is enough to completely close out surrounding land uses and at the same time attenuate any sounds floating in from outside.

The wall was plumbed and wired for a series of black granite shelves anchored into it, and from these flows a two-tier sheet waterfall. Inside this tight enclosure, the owners can throw open the large glass doors and make this outdoor wedge of space an extension of their living room. The high wall also keeps the bright, rippling sound of water inside the enclosure so it bounces off the surfaces to increase the ambience.

Here the simplicity of a mere semicircle wall evocative of a Frank Lloyd Wright application transformed the living room experience. The lacy bronze foliage

of cutleaf Japanese maple and the wall-hugging, diminutive leaves of creeping fig help tone down any glare from the white wall that reflects back onto large panes of glass. Nightlighting, craftily sequestered beyond and below the paving, shines up on the glistening black granite and during the winter silhouettes the barren branches of the finely pruned maples.

Construction was relatively simple and inexpensive because the wall was no more than common concrete slump block. A slurry of plaster gave it a smooth look and a pure white surface. Today, little of the white wall is seen except on the outside, under its cloak of verdant fig that reveals scant traces of what had been reclaimed from the street a few short years before. It illustrates the fact that one need not explore pricey materials to achieve the simple sophistication of high-quality design.

OPPOSITE PAGE, FAR LEFT The entry to this contemporary-style home was stark and cold. Michael brought the arching wall of the new front courtyard right off the corner of the building. To disguise the rather plain and rigid entry, Michael sought to make it more appealing with romantic plants that sprawl and dangle. The portico itself is cloaked in rampant wisteria vine (*Wisteria sinensis*), with the tangle of snakelike stems in sharp contrast to the precise wall, columns, and walkway. Likewise, the weeping Japanese cherry tree (*Prunus subhirtella 'Pendula'*) blooms at about the same time for a brilliant seasonal display. The reedlike fortnight lily (*Dietes vegeta*) combines to separate the tight entry from the garage at left. The ground plain retained the original lawn on one side of the walk, and the planter is filled with blue star creeper (*Isotoma fluviatilis*, or *Laurentia*) in bloom. **ABOVE** Inside the wall there is a truly miraculous transformation. The white wall has long ago been shrouded in shaggy evergreen creeping fig (*Ficus pumula*). This self-clinging vine is a bit too tender for cold climates. A suitable substitute is deciduous *Parthenocissus tricuspidata* (Boston ivy). The fig is often used in small-space gardens because it guarantees a wallpaper-thin covering for virtually any vertical surface, and it will grow out of holes in paving as small as 1 square foot (78 square centimeters). Often it is found on walls, in atriums, and in the narrowest side yards between buildings, where it thrives in the shade. Electric hedge clippers make trimming the vine in its later years a very simple task.

ABOVE The fountain that was once so visible is today shrouded in fig. Originally, each waterfall cascaded down in a single sheet, but the owners keep the fig clipped so that it interferes just enough to create a more irregular effect. The only visible vestige of the black granite tile can be seen on the flat surface of each tier, where the splashing of the water adds a certain natural dynamic to this otherwise well-controlled feature. It also provides an opportunity for recessed uplighting to illuminate the falling water from beneath. The shallow pool at the bottom is limited in size to take up the least amount of area possible. It is just wide enough to accommodate the waterfall without oversplash onto the paving. This dimension was carried around through the planters that mirror the curve of the wall. The bronze Japanese maples (*Acer japonicum 'Dissectum Atropurpureum'*) flank the water feature and add a delightful contrast of color and texture to the wall of fig. **LEFT** Amidst all these dark green and bronze foliaged plants, the white cherub stands out as the only decorative ornament. The fig has been allowed to entwine itself into the little statue, but tendrils are trimmed just enough to prevent complete coverage. The architectural ceramic tile is blue-black, and due to its frost resistance and high density it will not suffer damage or discoloring from the water. This view shows how much contact there is between the fig on the face of each tier and the water. If too much chlorine is added to this water, there can be burning of the foliage.

Raised Planters: What's on the Inside Counts

The great weakness of any kind of raised planter is water seepage. Over time, the water applied to plants and soils on the inside of the planter will travel through the block to weaken and discolor the surface plaster. It can cause irreparable harm, particularly in cold climates where the effects of repeated spring freeze and thaw wreak havoc.

Waterproofing is essential, particularly on light-colored walls. Those veneered with red brick, for example, will tolerate a considerable amount of seepage, and often the effects are quite attractive. But white or light-colored walls must be protected from the inside by waterproof membranes, hot tar, and other long-lasting sealants. Plus, water can never be allowed to accumulate inside the wall because even the best sealers can break down if they are overwet.

Raised walls must have drainage structures inside. This is more than just a few weep holes at the base of the wall. It is essential to use a French drain to gather any water accumulations and funnel them out of the planter efficiently. Employ a very experienced contractor who will ensure that there is sufficient drainage and sealant to keep this highly visible structure beautiful.

Water will always travel from an area of greater concentration to one of lesser concentration. This is the concept behind a *French drain*. Most applications involve drainpipe 3 to 4 inches (8 to 10 centimeters) in diameter that is perforated around its entire length. If you place this kind of pipe in the ground surrounded by saturated soil, the water travels from the soil (greater concentration) to the empty space inside the pipe, where there is less or no concentration. It then flows down the pipe and away from the area.

This drain is made even more effective if the pipe is surrounded by a few inches of gravel, a technique called *gravel packing*. The gravel acts as a filter to keep soil particles from immediately clogging up the little holes in the pipe. French drains are used underground in wet places that are poorly drained, or in conjunction with retaining walls and those of raised planters and curbs. They are placed at the bottom of the wall and run its entire length, thus draining the most critical place where water accumulates most and potentially wicks up into the masonry units, core, and face.

Waterproofing of masonry in contact with soil has come a long way in recent years. Originally, the best treatment was "hot mopping" with roofing tar, which was messy and somewhat expensive. Asphalt emulsion and roof patch are paint-on products that have been used for a long time. Some use newer kinds of paint-on sealers, but these have limited longevity (as does asphalt emulsion).

New durable plastics have produced waterproof membranes designed to be used in conjunction with masonry, lining the inside. They hold up indefinitely, but are vulnerable to gouging as soil is placed next to the wall, or when future gardening tasks are done in the finished area. Special "protector board" can be used to pad the membrane. Michael prefers to combine a waterproof membrane with a protective covering of board and a tar product.

Japanese maple trees of all kinds have been the favorite subjects of Oriental gardeners. When purchased well trained from the nursery, they will already have good form. These trees are kept free of excess twiggy growth that can fill up their silhouettes and destroy their beauty under nightlighting. Even the green, growing leaves are kept to a minimum so that the trees are always open and graceful, contrived so that parts of the branches are visible and thus appreciated. This illustrates one of the most important points of high-intensity small gardens: every inch of the plant will receive detailed inspection. There is no room for neglect of even the smallest details, both in plants and hardscape.

Profile: Santa Fe Transplant

It was well over ten years ago that Michael first encountered the run-down house on a golf course. His clients were the third owners of the home, but they had grown up in the same neighborhood and thus knew it personally. In its current state, the house belied its origins, but Michael knew it was unique and exemplified a time of explosive growth and the evolving ranch house style.

Plans for the house were originally designed by architect Cliff May, considered by many to be the father of California's postwar style. His work epitomized the casual style made popular by *Sunset* magazine in its most innovative years. Cliff May architecture essentially marries indoor and outdoor living spaces into a nearly seamless whole through broad openings in the walls, light-filled open rooms, and floor-to-ceiling glazing. His material choices were simple and earthy: textured

THE PSYCHOLOGY OF ARRIVAL IS MORE IMPORTANT THAN YOU THINK. IF IT IS NOT OBVIOUS WHERE TO PARK, IF THERE IS NO ROOM TO PARK WHEN YOU GET THERE, IF YOU STUMBLE TO THE BACK DOOR LOOKING FOR THE ENTRANCE, OR IF THE ENTRANCE IS BADLY LIGHTED, YOU WILL HAVE SUBJECTED YOUR GUESTS TO A SERIES OF ANNOYANCES WHICH WILL LINGER LONG IN THEIR SUBCONSCIOUS.

—THOMAS D. CHURCH, *GARDENS ARE FOR PEOPLE*, 1955

concrete block, rough sawn interior finish carpentry, exposed beams, slab floors with terra cotta tile, and detailing in stone, most often soft, rosy-toned Arizona flagstone.

The property values had skyrocketed since the beautiful Cliff May house was first built. The second owner, a designer, had changed the house before the real estate boom, and had used cheap materials that now were incongruous with the property value. The large story windows in front, designed to look out onto the surrounding golf course, had been hemmed in by a tiny courtyard and a dilapidated wood-and-iron fence. Bermuda-infested lawns and an aging asphalt driveway destroyed the grandeur that May had once envisioned.

The first step in the remodeling process was to review the original May plans that had come with the house. These showed the intent of the site layout and the architecture. May had suggested expansive courtyards with natural materials connected to those of the building. Clearly, there was little to salvage in the landscape.

The owners were frequent travelers and spent a great deal of time in Santa Fe, New Mexico. They were smitten with the style there and sought to transplant it tastefully to their new May house. With each venture into the Southwest, they brought back pieces of the style, such as weathered woodwork, sculptures, and even flagstone. Their intent was to remodel the house in phases, and each area would be created using their newfound materials.

The first order of business was demolition and removal of everything that did not belong to the original house. Lawns, fences, ironwork, concrete slabs, mow strips, lighting columns, and most of the foundation plantings were done away with. The palms, however, were salvaged for future use.

The owners were very interested in maximizing the indoor–outdoor connections as originally intended. As frequent travelers, they preferred a low-maintenance design, but enjoyed gardening when they were home.

The next priority was to create a grand sense of entry and redesign the original front courtyard to be four times its previous size. The entrance would feature double Spanish carved wood doors to bring it in scale with the surrounding open space. Its profile would reflect the stepped pueblo style, with a concrete slump block wall coated with a plaster slurry to give it a more adobe-like feel.

The cap material for all the walls was the pink Arizona flagstone milled into rectangular units with heavily textured sides. This simple detail would be carried throughout the entire project in all wall systems, be they seatwalls or barrier walls.

The new plans for the house re-created the circular driveway in a more compatible exposed aggregate concrete. The central planting island, originally flat, was improved with a matching curb wall of varying heights. This provided an edge against which the soil could be mounded to provide more interesting grade changes. This irregular topography made the boulders and dry streambed appear much more natural. The island was planted with a palette of gray-green plants so that the soft, muted hues would not compete with but frame the colorful gateway.

Inside the house, floors were covered with Saltillo pavers, the rustic 12-inch by 12-inch (36-centimeter by 36-centimeter) terra cotta tiles shipped in from Mexico. This material was extended outside so that there was a single continuous paving from the driveway through the courtyard and house to the back yard.

Inside the courtyard, the environment is quite different. You discover that the wall height is perfect to provide plenty of privacy but still allows you to peek over the top and see the expanses of green golf course beyond. The wall provides the backing for new raised planters, this time designed as seatwalls with wider caps. Whenever a raised planter is designed, it should be done in a way that allows it to double as seating. This is one of the primary techniques of small-space hardscape design: whenever you can build for dual duty, the result doubles your benefits. Seatwalls reduce the amount of furniture required so that there is maximum access around a minimal amount of tables, chairs, and lounges.

The courtyard is a very high-quality space that requires practically no maintenance. The raised planters allow each of the few plants to be wholly visible and appreciated from inside and out. There is no litter from overhanging trees, because shade is provided by market umbrellas. These courtyards can also be called "sun catchers" because they are outdoor living spaces in winter. The masonry enclosure blocks the cold winds; sun is reflected off the bright surfaces, warming the still air.

Another factor to consider if you live in a cold climate: how is the space protected in winter? The dilemma we often face is the need for shade in summer and the longing for warm sun in winter. Planting large trees is a very troublesome solution because of litter, root damage, and overall maintenance. Plus, even a deciduous tree creates shadows in winter. Block the biting winds, reflect the sun's weak rays, and avoid situations with moisture accumulation to ward off the dampness.

The chief feature of the front courtyard is the wall fountain, which was positioned directly in front of the dining room windows. It was a collaborative effort between Michael and his clients. The pink granite backing material is weatherproof and reflects the coloring of the flagstone, picking up red hues from the paving. A thin slot emits water over a cantilevered knife edge in a single sheet that then splashes on a school of bronze trout attached to the wall. They were commissioned by the owners from a Santa Fe sculptor.

TOP This corner lot had incredible visibility both to passersby and golfers on the course across the street. Clearly, May had planned a grand vista toward the course, yet it was cut off by the fence. **ABOVE LEFT** The driveway went right up to the gateway, with no opportunity to soften its appearance with planting. **ABOVE RIGHT** Inside the fence, the space was so tight that it was more like a small side yard between buildings than a courtyard on a huge lot with few limitations. **OPPOSITE** The front entry doors are the key to a sense of arrival at the Cliff May house. Using four wood panels, with just two that open, allowed for a grand arrival in scale with the rambling walls. The wall height rises over the doorway, which is framed by an exposed lintel and an extruded ridge that highlights it with additional shadow patterns. It is flanked by matched anodized copper wall sconce lighting fixtures that shine up and down to highlight the minute shadows produced by the uneven wall surface. This subtle illumination is made more festive through patterned openings in the face of each sconce. The walls extend outward on each side, with plantings located in raised planters to further enclose and emphasize the overall mass of the entry. The plants present exotic forms against the plain white wall. This drama and contrast through bronze foliage and unusual geometric shapes interrupts the extended masonry and enlivens the entire scheme. In the planter at right is the dramatic form of bronze New Zealand flax (*Phormium tenax 'Atropurpureum'*), and beyond that is the purple smoke tree (*Cotinus coggrygria 'Atropurpurea'*), a very popular Southwestern desert shrub. On the left is a nicely shaped Spanish bayonet (*Yucca aloifolia*), which blooms in white candelabras of waxy flowers that literally glow in moonlight.

RIGHT Many techniques were incorporated into the design of this wall system to make it more than a simple barrier or partition. The key is that everything varies. The center wall, 5 feet (2 meters) in height, is staggered at differing intervals. It provides a backing for raised planters, each at a slightly different height and depth. The exposed aggregate walk at the base allows absolute access to all planting areas and makes edging the adjacent lawn quick and easy. It also enhances the beauty of plants cascading off the planters so they do not compete with the greenery of the lawn. By the chimney is a weeping Japanese crab apple (*Malus floribundus*) surrounded by a carpet of white and pale purple sweet alyssum. The palm is a small-stature natural dwarf Mediterranean fan palm (*Chamerops humilis*), which tends to develop multiple trunks as part of its growth habit. The low-growing emerald green shrub spilling out of the planter is a native California lilac (*Ceanothus 'Carmel Creeper'*). The bright yellow flowers are perennial *Coreopsis grandiflora*. **BELOW RIGHT** The soft tones of the front island come out most beautifully at dusk. Rounded river cobble of varying sizes, from tiny pebbles to bread loaf, are arranged artistically to evoke a seasonal dry streambed. Large, angular boulders provide even more definition and interest. Overhead is the exquisitely pruned fruitless olive (*Olea europea 'Swan Hill'*), which exhibits the beauty of a specimen trained to multiple trunks. It is continuously pruned and shaped for open character to enhance visibility. The gray foliage groundcover snow-in-summer (*Cerastium tomentosum*) blooms in a continuous carpet of snow-white flowers in spring, and once these fade it can be mowed to renew the foliage. **FAR UPPER RIGHT** The low curb wall serves to retain soil at a new elevation. It is constructed to match the other walls on the site with the Arizona flagstone cap. Exposed aggregate concrete can be created out of different-colored pea gravel. This one was designed with more brown hues in order to better coordinate the colors of the driving surface with the flagstone. Recessed light fixtures define the edge of paving subtly during the evening, while fixtures are hidden beneath the trees to provide ambient mood uplighting after dark.

Arizona Flagstone

Granite and slate are very dense stones. They are efficient heat conductors, growing very hot and retaining heat for extended periods of time. In the west, where hot weather and balmy, warm nights are the result of seemingly endless summers, this thermal mass becomes a real liability.

In the 1920s, when building booms in California coincided with the sudden rise in population, new sources of locally originated flagstone were found in nearby Arizona. From the Painted Desert came a dense, colored sandstone that was reluctant to absorb heat or hold it for long. When used as paving, it would stay cool enough for bare feet and did not radiate the heat back into living spaces after nightfall like the more dense stones. In terms of practicality, this desert flagstone was easy to quarry, plentiful, relatively lightweight, strong, and cool.

It became the most popular poolside paving material west of the Mississippi, and its coarse surface made it naturally slip resistant. The flagstone was around my own grandparents' pool in Los Angeles, and I remember swimming there on very hot days. I often flopped down on the sunny deck in a wet swimsuit with the stone warm, but not uncomfortably hot. Arizona flagstone can still be seen in dozens of old movies.

The beauty of Arizona flagstone is unmatched by any other stone. Its color varies according to the quarry it came from, and the hues do reflect the rainbow of the Painted Desert itself. Bouquet Canyon flagstone is the darkest, almost brick red but a few shades paler. The lightest is cream-colored from the Kaibab Quarry, while the majority of the stock in shades of rosy pink fall somewhere in-between. The old pool decks used all the different types in a patchwork of different colors separated by a crazy quilt of mortar joints.

Paving today with Arizona flagstone is expensive. Most landscapes now use it as individual stepping stones or as an accent material. Michael makes the most of its heat-resistant qualities by using it as a comfortable cap on low seatwalls. It serves as a nice accent also on top of walls, where it is appreciated at eye level. As shown here, it is most compatible with Mexican pavers in dry landscapes.

BELOW This view of the trout fountain
from inside the dining room shows how
carefully aligned it was with the story
windows and door. Such precise respon-
siveness to the interior maximizes each
feature in the landscape to expand the
sense of space to many times its actual
area. RIGHT The trout fountain is a
contiguous part of the perimeter wall.
Its overall hues and textures match perfectly with the soft beige earth tones as
accents throughout the entire landscape.
Although quite simple, this is a bright
and active fountain capable of producing
enough flow and white noise to drown
out the din of the surrounding neighborhood. Note that when seated or reclining,
there is absolute privacy in this new front
yard courtyard.

RIGHT There are few openings in the paving for planting in the front courtyard because these
further reduce the living space. To screen off the entry doors from the fountain area, Michael
used twin square stone pots that can be moved around at will with the seasons and activities.
They are planted with young fruitless olives (*Olea europea 'Swan Hill'*), which grow slowly and
offer an open lacy screen. The teak patio furniture is allowed to weather and age naturally in
order to continue the rustic Southwestern character. FAR RIGHT Planting in the courtyard
emphasized color with a watermelon red crepe myrtle (*Lagerstroemia indica*), blooming yellow
daylilies (*Hemerocallis* spp.), and a wisteria vine pruned into a small tree. The purple bougainvillea
spilling off the front of the planter is actually too frost tender for this climate. The owner
loves it so much she treats it like an annual: because the growing seasons are so long here,
it can attain good size and bloom if planted from a well-developed container specimen.

How Phasing Works

Few people can afford to design and build their dream landscape all at once. This is especially true on large sites, because there is so much area to cover. But even small landscapes can be expensive, because high-quality materials and craftsmanship cost money. *Phasing* is a technique in which a project is done in affordable chunks.

There are some important guidelines to follow when phasing a project:

1. It's best to design the landscape for total buildout all at once, so that designer fees are kept to a minimum and you can break down the work into appropriate segments.
2. If you design the project one area at a time, choose a good designer and retain that professional for the duration of the project so there is continuity in design.
3. You can phase by completely building one part at a time, such as the front yard, back yard, courtyard, and so on. This method can be a bit more costly, because you have to start from scratch when doing each new area.
4. You can phase by completing each stage of the work independently, starting with the foundations and finishing with planting. Installation of a landscape is done in a particular order. If you interfere with that order, it can cost you a lot more money. Here is the approximate order, which varies according to the elements scheduled for that landscape:

   Demolition: Removing what's there and cleaning up the site
   Grading and drainage: Organizing the horizontal plane
   Pools and water features: Excavation, construction, and mechanical
   Paving, walls, and fences: Construction of footings and structures
   Irrigation and lighting: Installation of pipe, conduits, and fixtures
   Planting: Soil preparation and installation of every plant
   Finish work: Embellishments, furniture, and final details

Look closely and you will see a ghost of a channel in the tile where the sliding glass door track is hidden. Even the mortar joints of the pavers are aligned to reduce any sense of passing from inside to out. We transition gently from interior to covered exterior, then open exterior, and through the fence to the golf course beyond with the least amount of interruption possible.

Once inside, you pass into a single great room that opens out onto the back yard through floor-to-ceiling windows. The sliding glass doors here are 10 feet (3 meters) wide, a Cliff May technique that eliminates thresholds and changes in paving for a more seamless ground plain. Another hallmark of this architect's work is the sweeping roof line and multitude of skylights that ensure the covered area is never too dark, and overhead lighting for night. It is also designed to allow outdoor living and dining even in the wind and rain.

Originally, the central support post was hidden with plants, but Michael believed the best way to "make it disappear" was to ignore it. Beneath, the planter was filled in with Pebbletech (see page 97) for a waterproof natural surface and a unique fountain composed of pots and urns. These pots were ordinary Mexican fired clay with special antiquing by Michael's shop. It would not be wise to use actual antique pottery for this fountain, because the urns must be strong, thick-walled, and made of consistently dense clay to hold up over time. These were fully sealed on the inside to keep the water from seeping through and damaging the clay. Though it is not a spectacular fountain, it is one that is appropriate for giving a sense of moist coolness to this quiet shaded space.

The original swimming pool that existed when Michael first saw the house was freeform and located where the lawn is now. It was in the wrong place, and did nothing to enhance the beauty of the landscape. The decision was made to abandon it and build a new pool. The old one was busted up, torn out, and filled in. Originally, a new, simpler design was scheduled for its place, but the code did not allow it closer than 15 feet (5 meters) from the iron fence at the edge of the golf course. Safety issues that cropped up after the subdivision had first been built

LEFT This view of the pot fountain provides a better glimpse of the surface stones and Pebbletech beneath it. The pots need not sit on saucers, because underneath the stones is the reservoir and pump. The pebbles are combined with some flagstones for interest. **BELOW** The true beauty of this entire landscape is its simplicity. It is easy to hose down and care for, with large planting pushed back to the perimeter.

forced a change in the code to avoid golf ball accidents and to decrease the number of balls lost in residential swimming pools.

The only other location was to the side of the main patio. On one of their ventures to Santa Fe, the owners had found a marvelous monolithic modern sculpture made out of textured aluminum that was also a water feature. They brought it to Michael, who designed it into the landscape in a way that was fully responsive to the pool. It would sit in its own body of water, totally separate from the pool, to simplify the maintenance.

Now nestled in an alcove of the building where a main hallway opened onto the yard, he created a simple rectangular swimming pool, and at its far terminus stands the modern sculpture. The pool was lined with unique Pebbletech plaster for an unusual texture and natural coloring. Its coping material also came from Santa Fe, an abnormally thick flagstone hand-cut to give a rustic, chiseled appearance and resulting shadow patterns. Ever conscious of the smallest details, he chose a waterline tile that reflected the varying colors of the Arizona stone so that the entire composition would be fully coordinated.

The paving also changed from tile to broken flagstone in a narrow band around the pool. The downside to glazed terra cotta pavers is that they are far too slippery when wet to use around a pool. The flagstone used in these modest quantities looked better and was more affordable. To aid this transition, the owners asked for a small cactus garden at the edge of the patio. It would be surfaced with matching pebbles and planted in various species of barrel cactus that will eventually grow to be basketball size. Standing amidst these "eggs" are whimsical anatomically correct long-legged birds made out of scrap iron, plumbing fixtures, and tools allowed to rust and weather to a rustic patina.

BELOW The sculpture and the swimming pool are two independent water bodies in order to preserve the metal and overall water quality. Shown here is the juxtaposition and transition between the two types of paving. Note the absence of requisite foundation planting at the house walls, which reduces maintenance and allows the character of the architecture to show without competing with plants. **RIGHT** Still in its infancy, the cactus garden with its blooming "fishhook" barrels appear more like the eggs of these whimsical sculptures. **OPPOSITE** Here all the details are in perfect harmony. At the rear is the 'Climbing Joseph's Coat,' one of the few roses with all the hues of the desert sunset blooming on a single flowering shrub. Beside it is a newer striped cultivar of New Zealand flax, *Phormium tenax 'Maori Queen.'* As backdrop is the largest of the oleanders, white-flowering *Nerium oleander.* Espaliered on the wall is the evergreen pear (*Pyrus Kawakamii*) which becomes only partially deciduous during winter. This view shows how unique the sandstone coping units are, with their chiseled face and matching waterline tile.

Three tiers of roses are planted partly in the ground and partly in raised planters. The bottom tier is in natural soil and contains plants that spread out from the wall to gain mass rather than height. The middle tier doubles its capacity by combining plants of small stature with those trained into small trees. Upright grandifloras are on top, where they have excellent air circulation and unlimited potential to send their long stems upward and produce perfect cutting flowers.

The final feature of this lovely landscape is the rose garden. The owners are avid rosarians and tend their plants with parental care. As the perimeter wall sweeps around the far end of the house, it too is expanded with a series of step-down tier planters. These are on the outside of the wall, where golfers and drivers may admire their beauty. Filled with high-quality soil, they were planted with many kinds of everblooming roses: teas, floribundas, and grandifloras massed according to color. This is a remarkable space-saving technique; to mass this many plants on a single ground plain would require three times the space, because roses need lots of room and full sun.

All the roses are easy to water with a drip system, because they are in linear plantings. The wide flagstone caps on the walls make convenient standing places when tending and pruning the roses. With this southwest exposure, the plants receive sun all day. Roses do not appreciate shade in the morning, when it is crucial that the dew dry off the leaves as soon as possible. Lingering moisture is the bearer of the fungus diseases that plague roses.

Although the resurrection of this Cliff May house is not a small lot, it does contain many applications for limited-space gardens. The front courtyard claimed public space for private living and multiplied the visual size of the dining room. It makes a fine area for winter enjoyment with unobstructed afternoon sunshine. The rear yard is quite simple, with its unusual fountains, swimming pool, and sculptures. What Cliff May started, Michael Glassman finished in a wonderful composition that took over ten years to bring to this level of perfection.

Tricks with Pebbletech

This new product is an ideal way to provide a natural stone surface without the upkeep. It is used in various locations on this Cliff May house to evoke a desert environment. Pebbletech is a resinous fluid that is combined with river-rounded pebbles of virtually any size. It is poured into place and sets up hard. It's a lot like concrete, but the resin is perfectly clear. When complete, you have a natural surface that may be raked, brushed, or washed to remove debris without ever disturbing a stone. It can be used where there is water, as is the case in this feature, or in conjunction with swimming pools.

The relationship of the new front courtyard and its grand access to the circular drive is shown clearly here. The integration of the fish fountain into the walls and the juxtaposition of the various step-down planter walls reveal how complex the seemingly simple layout really is. The key is to identify the single core wall that runs the length of the entire enclosure.

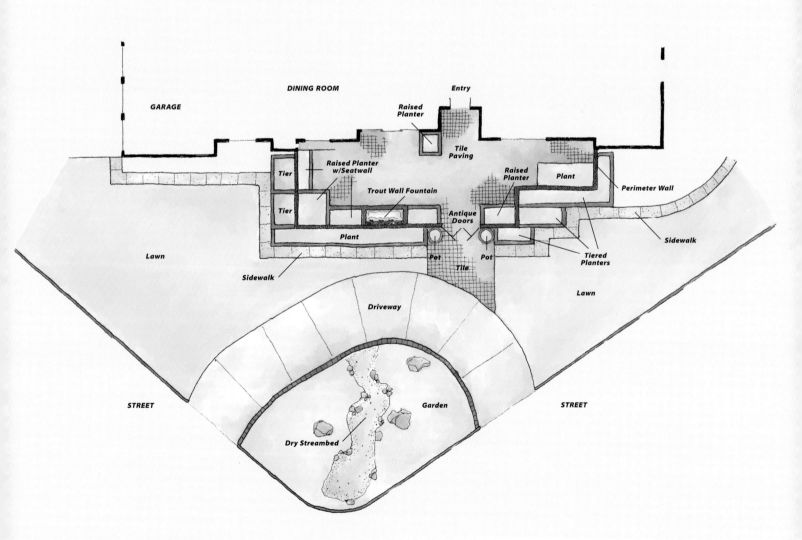

Pushing the Limit

It used to be a popular tradition to display the Christmas tree in your front window, where every passerby could appreciate it. In fact, the window became a view of the unused, sterile, rarely trod-upon front yards in an upper middle-class neighborhood. What was once a benefit is now less appreciated, for it tampers with privacy and sometimes home security as well.

Michael's clients came to him with such a home, opening onto the street. The west side was brutalized all summer long by the worst that the sun could aim at their windows. Few plants grew well, and the front door alcove became a heat sink during the dog days. Inside, the decor was sophisticated, Italian-European with rich fabrics and muted light, and the afternoon sun threatened daily to bleach out window coverings and carpet. The window view was uncomfortable, incongruous, and, frankly, made the carefully arranged interior mood look strangely out of place.

NO WAVING FERN-FROND IN A SHADY DELL IS MORE UNRESERVEDLY BEAUTIFUL IN FORM AND TEXTURE, OR HALF SO INSPIRING IN COLOR AND SPICY FRAGRANCE.

JOHN MUIR, *THE MOUNTAINS OF CALIFORNIA*, 1894

The neighborhood was strict about building codes. Turning this middle-class front yard into a private and sophisticated garden would take some careful planning. With the garage located farther from the street than the face of the house, there were few options.

When the codes fight you every step of the way, the only choice is to remodel the house—reset the parameters on your terms. There's no need to knock out walls; the way that Michael manipulates structures is to make them one contiguous whole so that the new face of the house is technically the same building, but visually separate.

To gain ground, he chose a Tuscan theme that would bind all details and materials. He designed a freestanding stucco entry portico that would stand over 20 feet (6 meters) beyond the face of the house and connect it to the original building by a lath shade arbor. It would aggrandize the sense of entry and serve as a point from which new walls could be built higher than the code limits, as they were now well behind the face of the portico, the new limit line.

The main feature would be a pair of hand-carved Mexican wood gates, mirroring the character of the similar front door beyond. Michael believes that all entry gates should be perfectly compatible with the house door so that the space flows as a coordinated whole. The solid wood doors also guarantee privacy that transparent gates could never match.

The new space he created would run along the entire front of the house and connect with the perimeter fence. It would be shaped like a dog bone, with the entry court on one end and a shaded dining area on the opposite end. The middle of the bone would run along the front window and serve as a strictly visual and transitional space.

The garden would have to be well shaded to thwart the afternoon sun, so Michael built two shade structures, one over each end space. They connected with

the house to a degree that allowed them to be considered part of the house. Both arbor overheads were painted white in order to provide plenty of shade without sacrificing light indoors. The dark brown arbors of the 1960s did nothing to enhance the beauty of spaces beneath them and actually proved gloomy, almost depressing, for overall lack of light. The idea is to provide shade and bright light, but no direct exposure.

The central transitional space has no covering so light bathes the wall and its lion's head fountain. The once sun-bleached living room window is shaded, except at high noon, and looks out onto the refreshing courtyard. The fountain mirrored the arched window with an imported Italianate Renaissance tile pattern that craftily arranged the color and geometry to suggest a three-dimensional effect. The basin below was constructed of stucco-covered concrete block to match the texture of the stucco walls.

The original front of the house can be seen behind the new portico. The design matches the exterior skin of the house and its tile roof. The raised relief on the front is a takeoff from the arched front window, a recurring motif throughout the garden. Walls project out on each side, now disguised by planting in the raised planters incorporated into the wall system.

ABOVE Inside the courtyard, the character of the garden is wholly different. Only the back wall of the portico is visible with the carved door open. This living space defined by the paving at the fountain is only 5 feet (2 meters) wide! That makes the small space transitional and the two end spaces more functional. Behind the door is the fern grotto—an impossibility with the harsh sun before, but now thriving beneath a simple shade arbor and protected by insulating masonry walls. Creeping fig (*Ficus pumula*) winds its way up the back side of the portico, and the fern grotto is filled with big leafy species. **RIGHT** The view of the lion's head fountain from the front room is one of complete harmony. The tones of the interior were carried into the fountain. Beyond the wall there is a screen of foliage that makes it hard to believe an ordinary middle-class neighborhood lurks just beyond it. The geometric connection between the front window and the fountain is perfect, and the flanking specially trained patio trees of potato vine (*Solanum jasminoides*), planted in antiqued ceramic pots, are carefully clipped into perfect topiary.

LEFT On the far end from the entry is a tiny space just large enough for a cast bronze art nouveau glass-top table and a pair of matching chairs. It is a cool green sanctuary for quiet reflection, where the wispy needled foliage of *Podocarpus gracilior*, tree ferns, and creeping fig blend into the refreshing chartreuse of babytears groundcover that threatens to engulf the stepping stones. The large tile pavers show the patina of age as well, with scrapes and stains and water marks all welcome additions to their texture.

BELOW LEFT The beauty of this fountain is the illusion of age; the sought-after patina lends character, as if the fountain were from another time and place. The fountain does not function as you would expect—the water source is actually in the shelf, and its flow is carefully controlled to fall just in front, and a small lip ensures it's not diffused by running off the sides. A black tile lip at the front prevents the water from sucking back onto the tile, falling freely and gracefully. This could have been an ordinary fountain, but it becomes a real artifact when faced in tiles that render such a creative three-dimensional illusion. Great water features need never be large, only perfect. **BELOW RIGHT** The focus of the little sanctuary is an Italian bronze sculpture of a young boy perched upon a carved marble pedestal. He is framed against the foliage-cloaked wall and the massive pillars that support the arbor. Gracefully draped behind him are the branches of firethorn (*Pyracantha coccinea*), a rugged shrub that bears brilliant orange-scarlet berries at Christmas. On either side are a matched pair of sago palms (*Cycas revoluta*), neither true palms nor ferns but primitive plants related to pine trees. Their unusually slow growth rate guarantees they will never grow too large for the sculpture in the owner's lifetime.

ABOVE A study in the greens of a natural dell, the fern garden is the most refreshing place of all on very hot, dry days. Here the old English love of the grotto is brought into the twentieth century in simple, contemporary terms. To the rear is a Japanese maple, straining under the constraints of wall and arbor. In autumn it will begin to turn, bringing a seasonal splash of warm color to this emerald cove. Despite the apparent diversity, there are only three ferns at work here. At center is the giant chain fern (*Woodwardia fimbriata*), a very rugged California native found in the moist stream canyons of the Sierra Nevada. Capable of withstanding considerable cold, snow, rainfall, and drought, it is a perfect large, upright fern for any application. Unlike the tree ferns, which grow taller with age, this one will never challenge the boundaries of the overhead structure. The stiff, upright fronds of the sword fern (*Neprolepis cordifolia*) are easy to identify. This is a unique spreading groundcover fern that travels quickly by underground runners. Although somewhat tender, these ferns are perfect container plants in cold climates, and, as they age and fill the pot, may be divided easily. The third species is strange and unusual among ferns, the holly fern (*Crytomium falcatum*), with its wide, stiff, and prickly fronds. The reedlike fortnight lily (*Dietes vegeta*) blooms among them with tall, wandlike stems that bear flowers akin to iris. And all is bound together with a verdant carpet of babytears. **RIGHT** A view of the fern garden from indoors shows the detail of a column fountain Michael designed for this garden. Its classical lines and the irregularities in the cast concrete texture are bold accents for the cool green background.

Looking Back on the Front Yard

Through these many landscapes, Michael teaches us that no problem is unsolvable. No matter how stringent the building codes, there are ways to get around them. We may remodel the house in clever ways to bring it closer to the street and thus buy space that we already own. We may enjoy the luxury of two front doors so that no uninvited visitor can look into our private home. A gateway and front door combined become a grand entry statement, one that transforms an ordinary tract house into something quite unique and special.

Walls are wonderfully versatile, providing not only enclosure, but the structural component for labor-saving raised planters. These, in turn, save us from purchasing outdoor furniture by doubling as comfortable overflow seating so we need not sacrifice an inch more than we have to. They can even become insulators capable of transforming impossible heat exposure.

The strength of masonry walls allows us to create fountains that include heavy components and creative stone, tile, and works of art without structural concerns. Walls may cost more to build, but in the long run they guarantee more space for living, privacy, security, and longevity.

Among the lessons of reclaiming front yards is that even a tiny wedge of added space can transform your living room view into another time and place, be it Renaissance Tuscany or old Santa Fe. Though it may be a challenge, with tenacity, know-how, and tricks of the trade, you can take control of what is already yours and make your front yard more than an ordinary window on the world.

The true "dog bone" shape of this front entry extension is revealed only in this plan. The orientation of a narrow, central transitional space links larger living spaces on either end. Positioning the wall fountain on the living room picture window makes it both an indoor and outdoor amenity. This location does not interfere with the usability of the two other spaces, proving that these lesser connections provide rich opportunities for visual beauty.

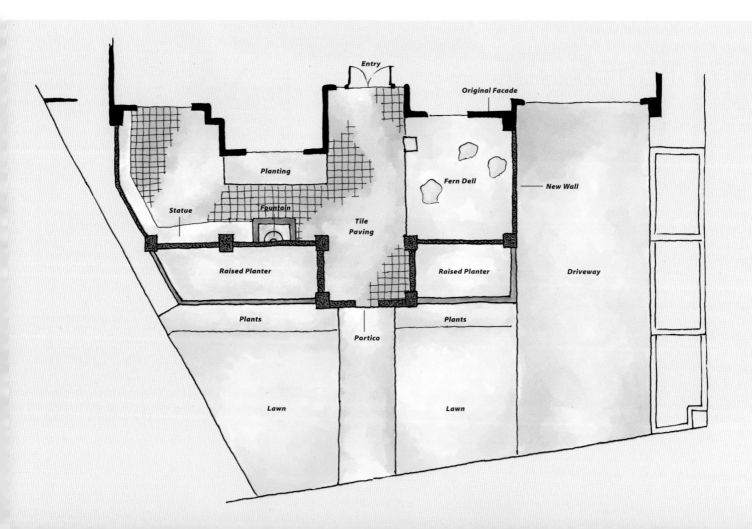

CHAPTER 5

TOWARDS HIS STUDY AND BEDCHAMBER JOYNES A LITTLE
GARDEN, WHICH THO' VERY NARROW, BY THE ADDITION OF A
WELL PAINTED PERSPECTIVE IS TO APPEARANCE GREATELY. IT IS A
VERY AGREEABLE DECEIT.

—JOHN EVELYN, DESCRIBING THE GARDEN
OF THE COUNT DE LIANCOURT, 1642

The Long and the Narrow

Solutions for Front, Back, and Side Yards

CALL IT A BOWLING ALLEY, A DRAG STRIP, AN OUTDOOR HALLWAY—
by any name, it is still a long, narrow space. Actually, these areas
can also be adjacent to streets, railroad rights-of-way, open space,
or a park. In each case, the unavoidable problem is that nothing
from the side yard may cross over the property line, whether it's a
monolith of a wall or an invisible survey line that marks the limit.

Long, narrow residential spaces exist more often today than
in the recent past because lots are shrinking. Less and less back
yard space is left over after the house is built; and where property

values are high, even these small areas can be a premium. Similarly, some homes have virtually no back yard at all, forcing homeowners to utilize areas that were not originally intended as outdoor living spaces. Front yards and side yards are now becoming gardens and entries, courtyards and play yards, for lack of any other option on the site.

Considerations for Long and Narrow Spaces

In many high-density subdivisions, there are homes with tiny strips of yard barely large enough to host a swimming pool. These landscapes are treated with the same spatial care that a true side yard is. These concepts apply to virtually any part of a homesite that's long and narrow, no matter what side of the house it's on.

When designing long, narrow spaces, it is critical that all the uses and needs be addressed. The importance of aesthetics cannot be overstated. In fact, these spaces tend to be primarily visual experiences as seen from indoors, even though more functional aspects may be there but out of sight.

Privacy

Neighboring houses (particularly two-story houses) can be a serious threat to privacy. The windows across the way might stare into yours, and since you often can't raise the fence due to code restrictions, your only real solution is to use plants as screening material. The ability to plant in the side yard becomes primary, so anything done there must allow for some kind of tree or shrub.

Visual Control

If you look at a typical narrow yard, you see only the far side of it from indoors. The base of the building wall is outside the view shed, which allows you to place practical features such as walks, utilities, and storage against the wall. The far side then becomes the aesthetic experience, planted and decorated to the hilt. In fact, if the planting area is raised up, you can see more small plants from the windows without looking down. It is this passive view, seen in a casual glance outside, that is most important, as it is the one you see every day.

Spatial Perception

In the quote that opens this chapter, the reference to "deceit" as being a justifiable design consideration is a noble one. For centuries, garden designers have perfected the art of illusion, using techniques that fool the eye into seeing more space than actually exists. The French developed the idea of creating flat panels with patterns in lattice that give the illusion of perspective to deceive the user into thinking more space exists than actually does. This is also achieved by murals painted on walls, and outdoor mirrors hung on fences or walls to suggest a doorway that reflects another garden beyond.

Enclosure

This approach applies more to open areas than those already enclosed with fences or buildings. The ability to enclose a piece of ground, no matter where it's located,

Privacy can be created within the side yard without the need for screen trees or shrubs. These windows each enjoy their own mini-garden environment enclosed by lattice fence panels covered in vines. Inside each are lovely works of art attached to the lattice at the ideal height for the window. This is an excellent technique for any city or high-density condition where big plants aren't allowed or the neighboring land use would not be suited to them.

defines the boundaries of that space. It's like homesteading, and this is most often used in highly exposed sites and corner lots where more than just one side of the house is open to street or open space. Enclosure not only reclaims space, it also sets the tone of the garden. Throughout this book are examples of how this is used in both front yard expansion and the privatization of other more exposed conditions.

True Side Yards

Side yards have always been the poor stepbrother of front and back yards. They are, for the most part, transient spaces, although a variety of permanent uses are the reason for their very existence. Size has a lot to do with their ultimate potential, as some are but 3 feet (1 meter) wide and others over 20 feet (6 meters).

Knowing how side yards function and the potential of wider-than-average side spaces help us to better understand how far we can push them to become something more. Perhaps of greatest importance to lifestyle and design is the fact that all the windows of that side of the house look out onto these places, which makes them visually part of the interior.

Connection is the primary purpose of side yards. They link the front and back of the house and serve as a transient area we frequently move through to one

This side yard contains a number of utilities disguised by the planting. A small gas meter squats up against the house. A hot water heater closet juts out from the building wall; behind it is an air conditioner surrounded by a nice short white lattice fence cloaked in star jasmine (*Trachelospermum jasminoides*).

Gates are important to side yards because they screen off storage areas. Their location must take into consideration access by utility meter readers. This example uses a double gate, scalloped to reflect the overhead arch, which focuses the view inside the circle. Roses make the overhead more attractive and take the emphasis away from the vent pipes on the rooftop beyond.

end or the other. Not only do we pass through, but we're often pushing a wheelbarrow or lawnmower, even a tote filled with firewood—all of which require certain clearances.

Side yards also serve as locations for utilities. Natural gas and electric utility meters are read at regular intervals for billing purposes, so they must be fully accessible. In most cases, they are located on the front corner of the house, but not always. This factor alone determines where a barrier fence, locked gate, or bushy hedge can be relative to meters.

Other utilities such as air conditioning units can be inside barriers, as they lack a meter. However, these big boxes must be serviced and repaired, so access remains important in a limited sense. These can't be moved either, so improvement of side yards must involve some creative disguise ideas.

Side yards are also used for storage. Everybody has to have a garbage can, but might not want to donate a percentage of the garage to these bulky and sometimes offensive containers. Other things stored outside include bikes, lawn toys, firewood, potting equipment, and a host of stuff we tend to accumulate but don't want to throw away.

Profile: When the Back Yard Thinks It's a Side Yard

Landscape design is ultimately a risky business when one seeks to travel beyond the commonplace and explore the realm of great and novel ideas. The risk is proportionate to the degree to which we trust our own skills and visions, for mistakes when laying out hardscape can be enormously expensive.

This landscape is inspired by the owner's affinity for the classical civilizations of the Mediterranean. Perhaps it would be best to take a glance at what these landscapes meant in history and the design elements that even today are still their most cherished legacies.

There beside that turquoise water of the Mediterranean Sea, olive trees changed the course of history. In Greek mythology, the city of Athens was named after the goddess Athena, who blessed the Greeks with the olive, a fruit from which oil was extracted. This oil provided the first consistently renewable source of fat and made the Greeks (and later the Romans) incredibly healthy and robust. It also fueled their lamps for study late into the evening hours. This, in turn, granted them enormous power and wealth well beyond all other civilizations in the West.

> ALL WORKS OF TASTE MUST BEAR A PRICE IN PROPORTION TO THE SKILL, TASTE, TIME, EXPENSE, AND RISK ATTENDING THEIR INVENTION AND MANUFACTURE.
> —JOSIAH WEDGEWOOD, POTTER, 1754

The architecture that emerged among the Greeks was a blocky post-and-beam technology. Not until the rise of the Romans did the arch appear, a perfect form of weightbearing construction that allowed far more latitude in building design. From both of these emerged the emphasis on the column, which remains with us thousands of years later.

What defines the column is the decorative capital on top, and sometimes at the bottom as well. It may be assigned to one of three main styles. The ornate *corinthian* capital was inspired by the flower of *Acanthus mollis*, a large-leaf perennial native to Greece and now found in American gardens. The *ionic* capital, shaped with matched spirals like the top half of a capital I, appeared in Greco-Roman architecture. Today only the simple *doric* capital is widely used, and its timeless beauty is illustrated by how well it adapts to a variety of garden styles.

A second model for this design scheme is inspired by the great waterworks of Renaissance Italian villa gardens. Villas dotting the hills of Italy took advantage of gravity to power a multitude of complex fountains that filled the old landscapes with the sight and sound of flowing water. These combinations of pools and falls are perfectly adapted to warm climates where the refreshing quality of water so greatly enhances outdoor spaces.

The garden that resulted from the integration of columns and water features into a small yard is one that employs virtually every opportunity to enhance visual beauty. The scene from every angle is equally beautiful because intimate attention has been lavished on details that make this landscape more than a garden. It is truly an extension of the interior, built by professionals but finished and planted by the owners so that the joint venture proves greater in whole than the sum of its parts.

The rear wall of the house, mostly glass, looked onto an extremely bright sunny space. The contrast proved too abrupt, and such direct afternoon sun promised to destroy furnishings indoors. To create the almost cloisterlike effect, a

The doric column, with its plain capital, is the most versatile for gardens, as it fits into practically any scheme. Here the row of columns evokes the post-and-beam Greek style of building. This is the view from the dining room onto the waterworks and the row of matched Italian cypress trees.

series of matched columns was used to support a shade arbor that is independent of the house though it may appear fully attached.

Just slightly longer than 50 feet (15 meters), and barely 30 feet (9 meters) at its widest, this landscaped space is divided into three separate parts. The first area is adjacent to the kitchen and living area, bounded by a gracefully curved masonry outdoor cook center that features an actual fireplace. It's odd to see such an application, but on those cool evenings of spring and fall it is as welcome to see cheerful flames outdoors as it is in the indoor fireplace. To reduce the tendency for the cook center to be perceived as a masonry-wall–like barrier, it has been cloaked in creeping fig (*Ficus pumula*) that the owners keep manicured to perfection. How incongruous yet dynamic it is to see a fireplace centered amidst a surface of green. The secret is that it is a gas fire, not a true wood-stoked fire. The gas prevents the surrounding masonry from heating up beyond temperatures tolerable for the vines.

The central zone is dedicated to the pool and spa complex. In this small area there are four full waterfalls, two that cascade off the spa and another pair on the opposite end of the pool. The matched falls adjacent to the outdoor dining area flow out of opposite sides of a long, elevated trough. The waterflow on all these features can be adjusted to the amount of sound and splash desired. The retaining wall on the far side of the pool is fitted with yet another creative detail, a series of spouts in the character of Moorish pools that shoot out into the main part of the pool. The sheer number of spillways combined with the jet streams makes this a most dynamic space, with water moving everywhere to effectively capture the Renaissance character of the Italian villa.

The far end of the garden is more passive and heavily planted because it is the major view

Nobody wanted to build the pool. All the contractors said my design was too complex, you just couldn't fit that many fountains in such a small area. Finally, we found a cooperative company that proved it could indeed be done. This shows how difficult it is when you come up with a new, challenging idea, because the contractors are only willing to build within their own familiar parameters unless you push them a little, and homeowners really can't do that without a knowledgeable advocate.

ABOVE LEFT The outdoor cook center contains all the amenities, but because it is cloaked in a clinging vine it does not appear to be hardscape. Actually, the effect is much like a hedge with a fireplace. The vine is creeping fig (*Ficus pumula*), which is a tender plant. In colder climates, either species of *Parthenocissus* (Boston ivy or Virginia creeper) will create the same effect. **BELOW LEFT** The outdoor dining area is just large enough to accommodate a table for six with enough room to circulate around it. No special treatment was given to the paving since the view contains so much interest. **ABOVE RIGHT** This fireplace is a more sophisticated alternative to the fire pit. More important, it takes far less space. It lends an unusual character to the landscaping, almost as though the garden was built around the ruins of an old castle or manor house. **OPPOSITE** The spa was raised up above the main part of the pool in order to allow the water to fall as far as possible. Note that the spillways are created out of stainless steel to make sure the cantilevered lip is sharp and clean. The surrounding masonry was finished with a pale pink industrial tile with a slightly irregular finish that reduces slippage. Using a very slick waterline tile in this condition would invite accidents.

ABOVE LEFT The little garden-esque corner was originally designated as lawn, but later was changed to the rose arch and angel of silence. Little boxwood hedges enclose the space and further the European feeling of the garden. **ABOVE RIGHT** The back fence came with the house, and the only change was the addition of the grid fixed to the face. This provided the perfect structure to support the lavender trumpet vines (*Clytostoma callistigioides*). A row of rose trees was planted here originally, but they were too small. The owners replaced them with these escallonia patio trees, which are kept sheared to perfection. This view also shows the second two-sided fountain, next to the dining area, where a 4-foot- (1-meter-) long sheet of water falls from stainless steel weirs.

shed for the dining area. A series of columnar Italian cypress trees (*Cupressus sempervirens*) is more evocative of Roman gardens than any other plant. It provides the perfect backdrop for the garden, blocking out the neighboring structure from the view with virtually no care required. In some climates, the English yew (*Taxus baccata*) makes a fine alternative. High-intensity color plants stand out against the dark evergreen background. This far corner is focused on a classical angel of silence sculpture atop a pedestal framed by an iron rose arch.

The remainder of the planting in this rear yard is concentrated against the fence decorated with faux verdigris grids of painted redwood, where vines gracefully crawl and drape. The row of *Escallonia fradesi* patio trees greatly contributes to the formal character of the garden. This glossy evergreen shrub, with its finely textured foliage, produces a topiary character that the owners need only shear occasionally to retain the crisp shapes.

The second part of this garden was built in a later phase in a bowling alley space less than 10 feet (3 meters) wide. The area ran along a highly visible wall of the house where windows to major living spaces had a dismal view of a dull fence and the neighbor's building on the other side.

The key to this space is what you see on the *far end* of the side yard. The same fence grid pattern extends along the entire side yard fence to increase interest in an unavoidable barrier. Overhead, a freestanding arbor structure screens off the walls of the neighbor's house and provides a trellis for flowering vines. The arbor was built inside a raised planter that runs between the fence and a narrow walkway, so there was no need to sacrifice space for posts and footings. Plus, the plantings cover up the post bases so they are barely noticeable.

The real gem of this side yard illustrates just how small a space can support a major water feature, which was centered on the dining room window. The raised planter was replaced by a fountain built to the same dimensions using beautiful marble tile veneer—again, a material found in classical architecture and sculpture. Water flows out of a bronze frieze spout with cherubs perched upon a slightly extruded shelf. To add even more drama, matched spouts set down into the water shoot streams from opposite directions for increased sound.

ABOVE LEFT The view from the side yard looking back toward the dining area gives a clear cross-section of the layout. To the right is the existing fence faced with grids. At its base is a raised masonry planter that contains the post and footings for the freestanding arbor covered with highly fragrant evergreen clematis (*Clematis armandii*). It is planted with Spanish lavender and hydrangea. The simple walkway is 3 feet (1 meter) wide, and on its left is a planter of equal width. **ABOVE RIGHT** This trademark of Michael Glassman's fences illustrates what a simple technique it really is. The wood panels are prefabricated in units painted in Michael's shop and then delivered to the job. Panels are attached with rust-resistant drive screws at post locations. Star jasmine (*Trachelospermum jasminoides*) is trained on this portion of the fence with garden penstemon (*Penstemon gloxinioides*) in the foreground. **LEFT** At the far end of the side yard is the fountain, fitted perfectly into a niche in the raised planter. It is really a low-maintenance water feature, as it contains chlorinated water that preserves its clear coloring and discourages algae.

This entire landscape was created with ordinary materials. The masonry is simple concrete block with a rough finish called *split face*. This surface texture produces shadow patterns and a stonelike texture without the expense. The nooks and crannies eventually become more interesting as algae and oxidation cause unique discolorations. If this effect is not desirable, simply acid wash the face from time to time.

The pink tile used throughout this project is actually an industrial product. Architects use this kind of material as "skin" on high-rise buildings because it is so resistant to damage and the color range is so broad. Such use requires it to be highly frost resistant, so the density of the tile makes it suitable for virtually any climate. Unlike residential tiles, industrial products can be obtained with a glossy surface, or with a slip-proof matte finish, as shown here. The key is to keep the tile color as close to neutral as possible so that it doesn't overwhelm the landscape.

It's unusual to find stainless steel applications like these cantilever weirs for sheet waterfalls in residential projects. These had to be done just right, or the water would suck back underneath toward the wall. The weir must be perfectly level, with a lip that is sharp and clean to ensure that the waterfall functions the way it is intended. In this case, the weir was fabricated with little fin walls on each side to funnel the waterflow so it does not split off on the edges and ruin the effect. This control is particularly crucial where pool lights are coordinated to backlight the falling water at night.

This Euro-clectic landscape is among the most highly designed small spaces in California. The degree of precision required for its completion cannot be overstated. From the original design work to the field installation, even the smallest error would have had an impact on many other parts of the project. The plumbing alone for the pool was a marvel, created so that any combination of waterfalls can be used.

There is little doubt that Michael has achieved what Wedgewood deemed essential to all works of taste. The skill of the designer and contractors was pushed to the limit. The expense was highly controlled to remain within the owner's limited budget. It is fortunate for us that this designer assumed all the risk of undertaking such an ambitious project, for only when we risk are we inspired to reach beyond the mundane and into the deep water of the avant-garde.

Ideas for Disguising Utilities

Homes are built with all sorts of utilities that are a part of everyday life. Some are public, which means they are installed and controlled by a city or public utilities district. Others are private—they belong to you and are under your umbrella of maintenance and repair.

Public Utilities

Every house has at least one meter, but there can be many, depending on where you are. In the city, there's electric, and perhaps natural gas too. Water meters are also part of the picture, but tend to be in sidewalks or under streets. Meters have to be read so that you can be billed for the service, which means there must be public access to each one. You can't block them off without incurring the wrath of the district. Second, these are the vital shutoff points where valves and break-

ers allow the service to be shut off manually. If you have a gas leak in the house, you must shut it off at the meter valve. The same applies if a pipe breaks and floods the bathroom. Public utilities can be disguised, but the technique must ensure that there is full access for reading and emergencies.

Private Utilities

The most common example of a private utility is an air conditioner, but sprinklers fall into this category as well. Air conditioners that sit outside on the ground have to have sufficient airflow, so you can't close them off. They also require service or repair, which demands free access on all sides. This applies to plants as well, because the repairperson can get awfully testy if he or she has to work around thorny plants such as roses. Sprinkler valves tend to be ganged up together; if they are automatic, you can disguise them with plants. Manually operated valves should be in the open where they can be easily turned on and off.

Some Additional Side Yard Uses

Side yards are also wonderfully practical and may become the only space available for storage, utilities, and even animals. The key is to provide for these practical concerns while maintaining as picturesque a view as possible for the windows that look out onto these liner spaces.

Dogs

We know that dog behavior in the home is more easily controlled when a space is provided for the pet. Indoors, a cushion or corner becomes the pet's home ground, where it feels safe and comfortable. Such is the case with a dog run, where a sizable outdoor area is given to run around in and use as a bathroom without withering plants or inflicting "female dog spot disease" on the lawn. This makes the pet more secure and the owner much more comfortable with the dog in the garden. Such areas should have some dirt or grass, plus an elevated area where the animal can be high and dry during wet weather.

ABOVE LEFT This electric meter was smack-dab in the middle of the back patio, forcing the meter reader to come into the yard. This lattice "closet" fence not only encloses the meter, but is tall enough that you don't even see the conduit coming down the wall. **ABOVE CENTER** If you want to cover up an air conditioner, low-lying meter, or crawl space, this short lattice fence is the best approach. For easy servicing, it is held together by pinned hinges that can be disassembled if extensive repair or replacement is needed. The lattice allows plenty of airflow and makes a fine support for climbing plants. **ABOVE RIGHT** Freestanding panels are great cover-ups for just about any unattractive utility, requiring little more than two posts and a prefabricated lattice panel painted to match the house. The little hedge at the base hides any footings or gaps in the bottom edge.

Recreational Vehicles

Rvs are rarely considered in design, but with more cities prohibiting the parking of unused vehicles on streets or in driveways, this is a growing issue. Rvs such as motorcycles, jet skis, campers, or dune buggies have distinct requirements for access and security. Theft is a concern in some neighborhoods, so security systems and gates are critical. Wherever a motor-driven RV is stored, there must be access to the driveway and a gate large enough for the vehicle to be parked.

Pool Equipment

The machines required to operate all the systems of a swimming pool can take up a lot of space. They also make noise and should not be placed close to windows or against bedroom walls. During the night they may turn on and off a number of times and can wreak havoc with light sleepers. Although existing pool equipment is rarely movable, new pools offer you the opportunity to place the equipment where it is not a visual or noisy nuisance.

Recycling

More and more people are becoming avid recyclers, but sometimes there isn't room for all those boxes and bins in either the garage or house. Side yards make the most convenient alternative place to keep them out of the rain. It's also easier to get them out a garden gate than doorways, and it will be wide enough for you to put it all in a cart or wagon for easier transport to curbside.

In this plan you can see how the living area was maximized by positioning it in the corner. It also shows the complexities of the pool and spa with the many associated spouts and fountains. From virtually any point in this garden there is at least one water feature in view. Note how narrow planters line the perimeters to reduce the visibility of fencing and distract from the neighboring structures.

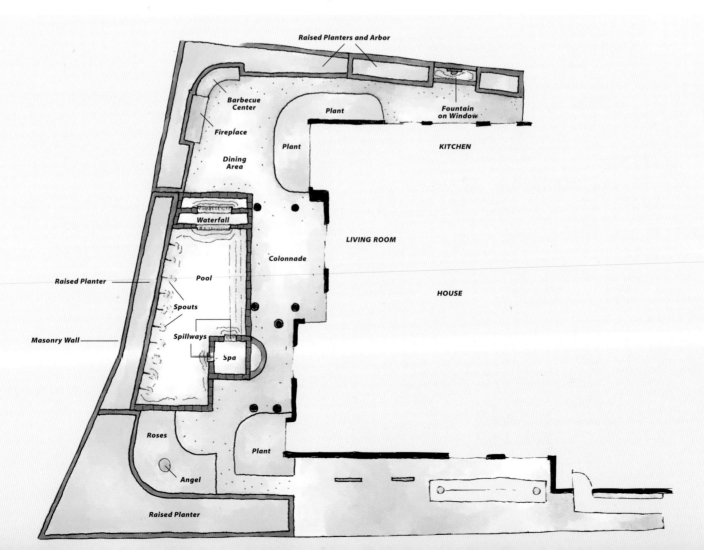

Profile: The Boxcar House

Thomas Church, a prominent San Francisco landscape architect of the early twentieth century, specialized in residential work. His contributions to our contemporary understanding of lifestyle-based landscaping finally buried the old notions of separation between indoor and outdoor spaces. Church's landscapes demonstrated that living in gardens could double the usable square footage of a home compared to the older approach of a garden as a separate entity suited only to frame the home architecture. In addition, the landscape could help to solve a lot of preexisting problems that made a home less usable.

This approach was totally lacking in a residence nicknamed "the boxcar house." Here was a two-story rectangular box painted brick red with coordinating pink concrete block! It seemed even taller than two stories because of solar panels perched on the roof. When it was built in the 1950s, it was a custom-designed contemporary house complete with an underground bomb shelter.

The whole architectural style shouted 1960s tacky, but the neighborhood had grown very desirable over the years so the value of the lot was considerable. The conditions found here are typical of what happens when the architect designs for efficiency and attention to the interior of the building. The result is that the outside facade, relative to the surrounding space, is not only ugly, it doesn't function well either.

> THE PHYSICIAN CAN BURY HIS MISTAKES, BUT THE ARCHITECT CAN ONLY ADVISE HIS CLIENTS TO PLANT VINES.
> —FRANK LLOYD WRIGHT, *THE LIVING CITY*, 1958

The boxcar house presented three serious problems:

1. The architecture had virtually no redeeming features and offered no opportunities for carrying motifs or materials into the landscape.
2. The front door was so insignificant that guests didn't know where to park and enter the structure.
3. As a corner lot, two sides of the house were open to the street, sacrificing a tremendous amount of land to public space; and problems with kids and dogs shortcutting the corner made improvements practically impossible.

The key to making this entire project come together was the construction of a fence to enclose as much of the public area as possible. This would stop corner-cutting by pedestrians and keep wandering pets out of the plantings. To do so, the proposal had to be presented to the city planning department in a request for variance. Michael felt that the only real way to salvage this land was with a 6-foot (2-meter) fence so that the entire area would feel enclosed and separate from the street. It would also be necessary to control the sense of entry.

What they proposed was a rustic, grape stake fence that would be semitransparent so that air and light could move through. This concept makes a fence more amenable to officials because it presents a far more attractive face to the neighborhood than a solid board fence. It was proposed at 5 feet (1½ meters) behind the curb to allow an attractive landscaping buffer, another important strategy for encouraging such an allowance. The condition officials fear is a fortresslike scenario that does not go over well with the neighboring properties that look over

TOP LEFT This view of the house's original front shows just how little there was to work with. The overly small windows, block and wood siding, flat vertical face, and a nearly invisible front-entry door offered little to make the home appear inviting or attractive. **TOP RIGHT** The neutral tone of redwood grape stakes weathers well and actually looks better over time. The landscape strip was planted in creeping red fescue combined with redwood trees that soften the blocky corners of the building. They also help break up the long line of fencing into smaller segments. **ABOVE RIGHT** A detail of the double gate and its arch, which line up perfectly on the arbor structure beyond. The transparent quality of the grape stakes gives a hint of what is beyond but offers a high degree of privacy to the occupants. The broad deck leading to the gate makes it clear that this is the point of entry, with boulders and nightlighting standards. **CENTER LEFT** Tiny details help express hospitality at the entry gate to this front courtyard. Placement is important so that the incised stone appears natural, not contrived. **BOTTOM LEFT** It's the little things that make a landscape unique. This gate uses a carefully chosen piece of driftwood as a "pull," which complements the naturally weathered redwood and bamboo.

From outside the fence there is little evidence to suggest that a garden exists inside. The gateway, when seen from within the garden, is a simple design, as are the overhead structures—but nothing in this landscape is symmetrical. The Japanese garden style abhors symmetry, as it rarely occurs in nature. Here is evidence that the same Asian quality can be achieved simply and can be enhanced with deodar cedar (*Cedrus deodara*), coast redwood (*Sequoia sempervirens*), different varieties of Japanese maple (*Acer palmatum*), and the serpentlike trunks of wisteria vine (*Wisteria sinensis*).

ABOVE LEFT Simple cedar tongue-in-groove planks were applied over the old masonry block, changing the character of the facade. Exposure to the elements has bleached out the coloring, lower left, while the upper right corner shows the original board color. **ABOVE RIGHT** Construction of the shade arbors was simple. Horizontals are double 2 by 6 lumber with the ends cut at a diagonal, a tradition in the Far East that lends a hint of Japanese design. It also eliminates the need for big, heavy timbers. Slats across the top are closely spaced 2-by-2s. The arbor was stained a pale warm gray so its presence would recede; a darker color would absorb light and seem oppressive. Babytears, mondo grass (*Ophiopogon japonica*), heavenly bamboo (*Nandina domestica*), and Japanese maple (*Acer japonicum*) grow under the arbor.

at this house. Fortunately, the city granted the variance, and the two long, narrow front yard strips were enclosed.

The difference in Michael's work is that he becomes a building designer as well as attending to the landscape. With a structure like the boxcar house, even the best landscape would be compromised, so the key becomes an integration of a new facade on the house that coordinates with the landscape style. Therefore, like vines, the poor architecture would be a cover-up makeover.

The first step in this project would be a facade makeover, covering the old concrete block with a chevron pattern of diagonal tongue-in-groove siding. The old siding, with vertical lines, was painted dark brown so it would recede, allowing the beauty of the new redwood to stand out sharply. These two simple improvements changed the entire character of the house itself.

Even with the new siding, the house was still a two-story vertical face. Therefore the goal was to bring this two-story scale down to human scale by creating projections that interrupt the wall. A series of simple wood arbors was designed to break up the vertical so that when standing out in front, one perceives the height as only that of the arbor instead of the roof much farther up. The arbors also shaded the face of the house and added character.

The new fence provided an opportunity to create a grand sense of entry. Since the door was jammed down on one end of the building, the gate was located where it would better suit the view from the street. Then the elevated wood deck guided visitors once inside through the garden to a surprise entry that lies in the

cool, shaded recesses of its own arrival space. The contrast to the totally open original layout is striking. The entire experience became intimately controlled from the layout of the walkway to the direction of the planking.

This entire landscape is integrated by a subtle rustic Asian character, which is finished by the creation of a meandering stream, which you cross over to enter the house. The water, plants, and other improvements make the narrow front strip into a stunning entry courtyard with its own garden experience. The owners like to sit out on the bridge in the evening and drink champagne. They keep the bottle under the deck, where it is convenient and kept cool in the running water.

The other leg of the landscape runs down the adjacent strip that now opens onto the breezeway. Before these improvements, there was no private lawn for family recreation, so the newly enclosed space became a traditional recreational lawn. A dry streambed that begins at the edge of the front water feature and runs naturally along the far edge of the lawn acts as a drainage swale. The arbors on the front of the house wrap around to this side, too, so that there is a lovely shaded seating area adjacent to the grass for adults.

What is remarkable about this landscape is partly that it reclaims the entire front yard, but more importantly that it shows how much garden can be poured into a long, narrow, bowling alley space. The once–sun-bleached elevation is now shaded by trees, verdant with plants and graced by the sound of water. What was once the boxcar house has become a garden setting that transformed this home from derelict architecture to dream landscape.

ABOVE LEFT The crowning glory of this front entry garden is the shallow streambed that runs its entire length. The water is treated with chlorine to keep it clear and algae free so that all the pebbles carefully placed in the bottom can be appreciated. The front door is at the far end of the path on the right beyond the planting. **ABOVE RIGHT** There is never any sign of concrete or plastic liner in this stream because large stones have been carefully placed to give it a clean but natural edge. Asparagus fern (*Asparagus sprengeri*) creates a soft buffer of bright green along its length. The deck is only inches (or centimeters) above the waterline, showing how little gap is required to create bridging with the deck.

Side yards often run along barren garage walls lacking windows for relief. Though a side yard is not immediately visible from inside the house, it is still a part of the land-scape. Espaliering evergreen pear (*Pyrus Kawakamii*) is attractive and requires just 6 inches (15 centimeters) of space along the face of the wall. This espalier will turn snow white when in bloom come spring.

Tunnel Vision

Side yard conditions can occur anywhere, because they constitute a situation, not a strict definition. They can occur in the front yard or in the back, because the long and narrow is treated with the same techniques. The key to all these scenarios is to begin with what you see, consider how you want it to function, and then explore how to control the impact on users. Then you can go beyond garbage-can storage and into the tight constraints of a stream, a swimming pool, or a fountain. When space is on the short side and you have to make every inch count, never let the long and the narrow stifle your creativity—and remember all that can exist in those forgotten strips of earth we collectively call side yards.

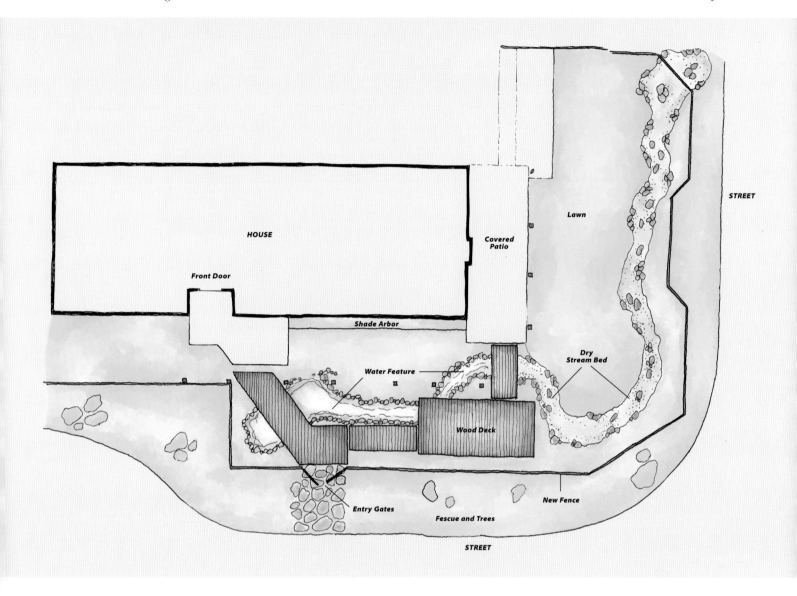

The relationship between the new gateway and the hidden front door is easily seen in both this plan and on the ground by the alignment of the deck. The deck also conveniently connects the entry to the now semiprivate enclosed lawn area. The water feature works in tandem with the deck to logically transition into the dry stream bed and lawn without abrupt changes.

CHAPTER 6

IF WATER CAN BE PROJECTED INTO THE SKY TO CAUSE ETERNAL SURPRISE AT SUCH FINE ARTIFICE, OR BE ALLOWED TO SPLASH DOWN LIKE A CONTROLLED WATERFALL, IT CAN ALSO LIE STILL AND QUIET, A MIRROR WHEN THE SUN SHINES OR A SUGGESTION OF UNPLUMBABLE DEPTH UNDER LEADEN SKIES.

—MILES HADFIELD, *THE ART OF THE GARDEN*, 1965

Fountains and Water Gardens

Artistic Designs for a Fluid Material

THERE ARE NO NEW IDEAS; ONLY THE APPLICATION OF IDEAS CHANGES. This truth is acknowledged by all designers, because history holds the greatest and most widely proven ideas. It is up to us to discover them and try new adaptations in contemporary gardens. Nowhere but in the world of fountains is this so apparent.

Since the great wells were constructed in the hanging gardens of Babylon, and later the highly engineered waterworks of Versailles and Villa Lante, there is little doubt that since ancient times fountains have been a coveted element in gardens. These feats of

This large shade garden required a larger fountain that would remain in scale. It is a Spanish style, but rather than overflow, the water flows out small spouts in the upper reservoir along with a spout on top. This fountain has a very narrow base that allows babytears and impatiens to be planted all around the bottom to cover the bottom edge. This shows how much the planting can enhance the beauty of fountains. The four-quarter design of the spouts is mirrored by potted spider plants on top of flat cast concrete disks.

Old World engineering were massive constructions fed by endless aqueducts for gravity-fed pressure, and until recent years, the complications of building water features in home landscapes made them strictly for the very wealthy. Today, there are so many new ways to use water that opportunities exist for every site and every budget.

Waterworks are great additions to any garden. They give life and animation to dead space, and dramatically change the character of their surroundings. Water is a lure for birds, which are not only charming to behold but also help control pests in your garden. And at night, there is nothing quite like a well-lit fountain to make outdoor views from inside the home more than just a glance into the dark.

ALL FALLING WATER DOESN'T SOUND THE SAME; AND NO TWO FOUNTAINS SOUND EXACTLY ALIKE. EACH HAS A DIFFERENT EFFECT, WHICH DEPENDS, ALSO, ON THE ACOUSTICS OF ITS LOCATION IN THE GARDEN. INDIVIDUAL PREFERENCE IS ALSO A FACTOR—WHAT ONE FINDS SOOTHING, ANOTHER FINDS ANNOYING. OTHERS PREFER SILENCE, AND ENJOY THE WATER FEATURE AS A STRICTLY VISUAL EXPERIENCE.

—MICHAEL GLASSMAN

Integrating Water Features into Small Gardens

If you watch people wander around public gardens, they will invariably choose to rest beside water features or sit and look upon pools or fountains from a certain vantage point. Certainly, being close to water appeals to a primitive sense, while a broader perspective may be a response to the sheer beauty of water in the landscape. It also points out that water in a garden may be designed as part of the view shed, or something to be experienced intimately within the living space itself.

A view shed water garden should be of sufficient size to be in scale with its surroundings and to ensure visibility from the living space. Designs should be simple and expansive, with artistic embellishments bold and easily discernible. Fussy detailing from a distance is usually a wasted effort.

Those water features in and around living spaces will receive far greater scrutiny. Every inch may be studied as you dine or sit in the sun, and if there is a lack of attention to fine detailing, the ragged edges will come back to haunt you on a bright, sunny day. It's also important in smaller gardens to avoid oversizing the water features. This is partly because it claims too much precious living space. No water feature is so important that its right to space exceeds that of the user. In addition, tight spaces allow you to create tiny pools and waterfalls that produce far greater benefit than their size would suggest.

Waterfalls and fountainheads should be carefully designed to be the primary focus of the feature. Prefabricated fountain units are used in small gardens to conserve usable space for people, which is the simplest way to create a water feature. It's important to match the style of the fountain to that of the house, but when architecture is ambiguous, keep things simple. If you do have thematic architecture and are unsure of a design, hire an expert to help with the selection. There are many possibilities for Asian-inspired gardens, and just as many Spanish and classical motifs. Naturalistic art nouveau is one style that tends to respond more to the surrounding garden than architecture, because it is rooted in natural motifs.

Beware if your garden or fountain site is persistently windy, a common condition along coastlines and in some inner cities, where tall buildings can create wind tunnel effects. To reduce the chance of overspray, avoid fountains that produce a fine mist, because the wind will either cause a high rate of evaporation or the area downwind will be perpetually wet. If a patio is downwind, you can expect mineral buildup or discoloration of paving and bleaching of wood fences, deck, or siding. Above all, no one will want to sit there, which forces you to sacrifice precious living space.

This illustrates why you should pay close attention to the kind of spout you buy. Even more valuable is the ability to adjust the flow by hand, which not only mitigates environmental problems, but also lets you decide exactly how much sound you get. It's nice to be able to turn it up while noisily entertaining and then turn it back to a trickle for a quiet afternoon rest in your lounge chair.

Fountains and water features are always more attractive when surrounded by plants. They make the entire environment appear more natural. Some fountains have cords and other paraphernalia that need to be disguised, and plants are the ideal cover-up.

Water Gardens and Water Features

Garden water features fall into two main categories—water gardens and water features—and each is treated in a very different way. You must know what you are trying to achieve before you design or buy a water feature, because they have very different requirements.

A *water garden* is just that, a garden of plants that grow in the water. The plants require at least four hours of sunlight to grow well, so shaded locations are not the best exposures for this application. Water garden plants include those that are aquatic, such as water lilies. There are also marginals, which live around the edges of the water and are adapted to both wet and dry conditions. Marginals are mostly reedlike plants such as the butterfly iris (*Iris ensata*). Water gardens often include koi fish and other types of aquatic life that feed on unwanted algae.

The second category is *water features*, which are purely decorative. They are sterile and contain no plants or fish. Like swimming pools, they can be treated with chemicals to keep the water clear and sparkling. You can build these anywhere on the landscape, because they do not require sunlight. They are less challenging to care for because there are no fish to feed, nor is it necessary to circulate the water for the health of the fish.

Both water gardens and decorative water features are built the same way, with a few important differences. For example, certain plant types won't grow if the water is too shallow or too deep, and in hot climates the water may overheat and kill fish if it isn't deep enough. Plus, special filters are required for water gardens to control organic matter accumulations in the water—but in general, the shell and mechanical pumps are similar.

In-ground waterworks are built much the same as a swimming pool, by lining an excavated hole with material that keeps the water from seeping into the soil. A waterfall of some sort is required to help aerate and circulate the water (and it

An ugly cut slope adjacent to a dining room provided the perfect change in grade for a natural water garden. Hidden amidst the rocks is a simple water hole, fed from the rock shelf above, which is all that's required to support water lilies and horsetail (*Equisetum arvense*).

A large wall supports this elaborate lion's-head fountain created in lovely decorative color tiles in the Spanish style. This sun-drenched patio reflects the light brightly, and each of the cantilevered tiers sheds its overflow in a different way. Heavy waterflow produces plentiful sound in this walled garden. The setting is perfect for the dark green vines and terra cotta pots.

looks good, too!). This construction is considered permanent—so if you get tired of it, short of jackhammers, there's no other choice but to fill it with topsoil and make it a planter.

Style Options

You can separate waterworks into formal or informal designs. Much of the character is derived from the shape of the pool itself, which is further supported by the nature of the waterfall or spout.

Formal designs tends to be rigid, in simple geometric shapes such as a circle or rectangle. Designs are gleaned from the classical style of Roman baths or sculptural fountains. The sleek, modern, swimming-pool–like layouts common in contemporary homes are even simpler, although the waterfall systems can be deceptively complex. Formal water features utilize regular-sized masonry units such as block and ceramic tiles.

Informal designs tend to be irregular and freeform. They are inspired by models found in nature such as a tropical lagoon, forest spring, or river rapids. It's common for informal pools to be created with poured concrete and lots of rocks, from boulder-sized to gravel.

Pools, whether formal or informal, can be still and glassy, with the surface reflecting the sky and the surrounding landscape. More dynamic designs include fountains and waterfalls that move continuously and assert themselves more boldly into the senses of the viewer.

With all these options to choose from, your budget may prove the most powerful deciding factor. The natural pool might be created out of a rigid prefabricated fiberglass shell that you simply bury and fill, saving thousands of dollars over the pricey concrete version. Granted, it may not last as long, but then again it's easy to replace. Keep in mind that the reason water features in home landscapes have exploded so largely on the garden scene is because of these shells and inexpensive plastic pumps. So whether it's formal or informal, a water garden or just a fountain, any version is a welcome improvement to a static, dry garden.

Basic Components of Water Features

Each water feature is a unique creation, as is each landscape. Depending on the scale and complexity, it may include a number of different components, each just as important to the overall success of the pool. Water features that are dynamic and circulate require a pump and other mechanical equipment. For an elaborate in-ground waterworks, you'll have to install drains, pumps and filters, all of which require an experienced professional.

Shell

All in-ground water features must hold water, which necessitates some sort of barrier to prevent it from percolating down into the soil. Barriers are made out of various types of materials that vary considerably in price, so you must choose one that fits your pool size, shape, and depth. It must also be compatible with the local climate conditions, which is crucial if you live where the ground freezes in winter.

Leaks Are Nightmares

The single problem that most afflicts in-ground water features is leaking. Leaking can be very gradual, but the cumulative effects can create a serious liability for the homeowner. Leaks can also be expensive, because they waste water. Worse yet is the potential for undermining the pool, and water pooling underground can drown nearby plant roots while the soil surface appears dry. Subterranean leaks can also travel underground to the neighbor's yard.

Leaking can be caused by a variety of factors, from sloppy workmanship to earthquakes. Liners set right on the soil are a common mistake, because the weight of a full pond of water can be enough to tear the plastic where it contacts rocks or other extrusions. One good way to keep this from happening is to use many layers of old carpet padding as a cushion under the liner or fiberglass shell, since the carpet padding is soft and resists decomposition. But even the most meticulous installation cannot guarantee against all leaks, which is why Michael insists on the architectural sandwich of liner, concrete, and sealant.

For in-ground units, the cheapest route is a rigid fiberglass shell or a flexible plastic liner. A shell limits you to whatever size and shape is available, while a liner can be used for pools of virtually any size or shape. You simply dig a hole and line it with the plastic, then anchor it around the edges, and it's ready for water. For either type, liner or shell, it is important to the product longevity to protect the edges from sunlight, which will, over time, degrade the material. Choose some stone for the rim to cover up the ugly edge of exposed plastic. Essentially, that's all there is to it.

In-ground concrete-lined pools are sometimes nearly as costly as a small swimming pool or spa. The weight of the water upon the structure combined with the ravages of weather and time can inevitably cause stress fractures. There must be adequate insurance that the money spent to build the pool is worthwhile over the long term.

Michael recommends an architectural sandwich, or layered liner, that is suitable for warm climates but may require adaptations for extreme winter conditions. In short, the goal is to create a permanent pool that will not leak and is strong enough to bear the weight of dogs or repairpersons who may need to work on it in the future. The shell must not only be durable, but beautiful too.

The architectural sandwich begins on the floor of a newly excavated hole, which is dug much deeper and wider than the expected bottom of the pool to allow for the thickness of the shell construction. The first layer is sand, which helps accommodate the expansion and contraction of soil. Then a plastic waterproof liner is installed, followed by steel reinforcement rods and plumbing for the drain, filter, and water circulation. Then the concrete shell is poured and finished by hand. Once it has cured, the pond is filled and tested for leaks. Then, if it passes, a masonry sealant is applied to the concrete to fill the pores.

Pumps

The kind of pump you use relates to the amount of water you circulate in the pool. Even if you don't have a waterfall or fountain, you must still have a pump, because moving water, even it it's barely inching along, discourages algae in water gardens.

If you are pushing less than 4,000 to 5,000 gallons (15,200 to 19,000 liters) per hour, you can use a submersible pump. These are preferred for small-space gardens, because you need not dedicate a place for the pump. Submersibles can be hidden at the bottom of the pool, and the water serves as a noise-reduction insulator that muffles the characteristic hum of the pump when it's operating. Choose only brass and stainless steel submersible pumps because they have the longest life span and come with a long-term warranty.

For bigger water features and pools that require a flow rate greater than 5,000 gallons (19,000 liters) per hour, use a dry pump that's positioned outside the water. These are also called *swimming pool pumps*, which gives you an idea of their size and the amount of noise they make. Their strength ranges from 1 to 2 horsepower, which moves huge amounts of water—crucial to powering big waterfalls.

It's always a good idea for large in-ground concrete pool waterfalls to have the entire water feature professionally designed. This ensures that the pump is adequately sized for the effect you have in mind. The engineer will take into consideration three factors designated on the plan: feet of head, rate of flow, and volume.

First is the *feet (meters) of head*, which indicates how many vertical feet (or meters) you must pump the water to get it over the top of the waterfall. Second is the weir size, which dictates the minimum speed or *rate of flow* required to make that waterfall flow properly. Third is the *volume* of water you want to push over the weir at a certain depth, such as 1 inch (25 millimeters) or 2 inches (50 millimeters) deep. The engineer will establish the range of an adjustable pump to properly accommodate its minimum and maximum rate variation.

Controls

All water features have controls for on/off, flow rate, and sometimes lighting. If controlled at the fountain, always use ball valves or gate valves to allow you to easily control flow rates and sound. Make the valve easily accessible so you don't have to step into mud or wade through plants to turn down the fountain.

You can also take advantage of remote control systems like those you use for your TV. This eliminates the need to run wires through house walls. It's crucial to be able to control the functions from indoors as well so you don't have to go out in the rain in your Sunday best to turn on the waterworks.

Lighting

Without artificial lighting, all landscapes and water features would be swallowed up by the night. In the darkness, the greatest beauty of moving water is revealed by illumination carefully contrived to enhance its sparkling qualities. *Ambient lighting* is a technique of placing lights so that their source is never discernible, but they offer widespread illumination. Nobody wants to see the fixture, only the effect.

Uplighting and *downlighting* do not describe the fixture, but a technique related to the direction of the light source. Uplighting shoots upward from underneath, while downlighting shoots down from far above. Each has its own benefits and liabilities, but a well-illuminated water feature utilizes both.

Downlighting illuminates the entire feature and is important when using sculptural fountains that can be made more three-dimensional by light and shadow. Fountains with water shooting out of the top rely on this technique to shine through every drop and send prisms of color bouncing off every particle of mist.

This landscape is a study in ambient lighting, and you would be hard-pressed to find the source fixtures. Uplighting has been hidden in the plants at the base of each column, making the carefully trained vines cast dramatic spiral shadows. The face of the fountain is lighted by bullet fixtures hidden on the back side of the overhead arbor beam. The pool utilizes enough underwater light source that the spout streams stand out clearly against the darkness.

Spotlight fixtures for downlighting can be mounted on any surface above the water feature such as walls, trees, or shade arbors. It is important that the light itself be hooded, so that a narrow beam is focused directly onto the fountain. Open light fixtures become a distraction, because their source of light will appear far brighter than the subject illuminated, destroying the entire effect. High-intensity halogen bulbs in tiny fixtures are recommended, since these are less visually obtrusive during the day than larger bullet floodlights.

Uplighting allows you to be more creative. Newer low-voltage waterproof fixtures are made out of brass and stainless steel to avoid corrosion. These units are attached to the end of a cord you plug into a 110-volt outlet. Simply drop the fixture into the water basin of the fountain and position it to shine wherever you wish. The only limitation to these fixtures is that they must remain fully submerged while operating, or they will quickly overheat and explode.

This kind of lighting is particularly valuable for wall fountains, because the fixture is hidden in the basin to shine up and illuminate the single stream of water shooting out of the spout. The light also highlights the relief of the back panel to make these designs more visible at night.

In-water lighting is ideal for any other kind of fountain as well, be it a Spanish tier fountain or a simple ceramic pot water garden. It is important to route the cords so they are invisible during the day, which may require some creativity. Another application for waterfall units is to place the fixture behind the water to backlight fountains and waterfalls for a glowing sheet of water.

For larger, permanent water features such as natural pools or swimming-pool–like constructions, it is best to use 110-volt swimming pool lights. Though they are expensive, no 12 volt unit can produce enough illumination for these larger applications.

This beautiful bronze sculpture is downlighted by a tiny light mounted on the house wall just above the window. At dusk or night, the small stream of water would be invisible without such focused illumination. These inconspicuous fixures are adjustable, allowing you to fine-tune the direction of the spot.

Landscape Electricity and Safety

Safety is the primary issue concerning all things electric used outdoors. The water and accumulated moisture that exist outdoors and are associated with water features of any kind are a recipe for disaster. It is highly recommended that all electrical components associated with lighting and pumps be installed or approved by a licensed electrician. Your life depends on it.

Landscape electric can be broken down into two types:

One hundred ten-volt electrical components are just like those in your house. In short, they can shock the hell out of you. When used outdoors, they require conduit, junction boxes, and waterproof switches and plugs. Pumps and filters require 110-volt connections whether they are plug-in or hard-wired. All should be installed by a licensed electrician.

If you wish to install a fountain that is not close to an outdoor 110-volt outlet, do not run extension cords across the yard. It is strongly recommended that an electrician lay conduit to the new fountain location and provide an appropriate outlet there. Whenever possible, cover the outlet to keep the connection of the pump cord to the receptacle dry and protected from rain, sprinklers, or overspray from the fountain itself.

Twelve volt is for very low-voltage systems that are plugged into 110-volt outlets located indoors, or into outdoor waterproof plugs. A 12-volt is so easy and safe that you could virtually bite down on a live 12-volt cord and it would barely shock you at all—but don't try this at home. The difference between 12-volt and 110-volt can be life and death.

ABOVE RIGHT There will be a small fountain and lighting associated with this little raised planter garden and it has just been wired by the electrician. It is connected to the house circuit breaker panel with a ground fault interrupter. What you see is the conduit sticking out of the ground, topped with a junction box that contains a duplex outdoor waterproof plug. Building codes require junction boxes to be at least a foot (30 centimeters) above the surrounding soil to ensure they remain high and dry and safe.

ABOVE LEFT This is the same little garden after completion. Note the French water spout now at the center of the garden. It is used to cover up the junction box with something both attractive and practical.

The beauty of a simple little brick planter is enhanced dramatically by a simple one-tier fountain that is perfectly in scale with its surroundings. The wide pool is set on a bed of leveled gravel. The finish is a verdigris copper topped with a pineapple motif, once the symbol of hospitality.

Fountains

Fountains in the garden can be one of the most exciting and animated elements in a landscape. The movement of water sparkles in sunlight and creates beautiful sounds that are subconsciously soothing. The great gardens of history show us how fountains can be integrated into practically any design style, but as always the water feature must be in scale with its surroundings. The design of the fountain should also complement the design style of the rest of the garden, which means that color, motif, and function will make it part of the overall scheme. If you fail to achieve this, the fountain will stand out and appear more as an afterthought than an integral part of the design.

Unit Fountains

Prefabricated fountain units are affordable and simple to use—you just set them up, fill with the garden hose, and plug in the pump. Hidden inside the base or behind it are small pumps that circulate the water. There are simple birdbath pedestal-and-bowl types or elaborate multitiered Spanish units. Wall-mounted Italian fountains are part of this group as well. There's a great deal of choice in sculptural motifs and finish colors, making it a challenge to pick out just the right one.

Tier Fountains

People generically call them Spanish fountains, but the single aspect tier fountains share is a series of two or more stacked tier pools. The top pools are narrower than those below them so that each overflows into the next one down. This kind of fountain is the most adaptable because it is manufactured in stackable pieces. It can be made out of cast concrete or expensive carved stone. Since the pools are shallow, those that feature just one pool are often called birdbath fountains because they do attract birds in great numbers.

Far more ornate is this baroque-style cherub tier fountain that is abnormally tall and narrow but reflects the very tall, multistoried building wall. This kind of detail and the white coloring of the fountain are not appropriate everywhere.

ABOVE RIGHT This classic wall fountain is newly installed on a garage wall. It's made far more beautiful by the surrounding oval frame and grid trellis. Passionflower vines are being trained up and around so that eventually it will be nestled in a bed of foliage and not appear in such stark contrast. The electrical connection was routed through the wall behind and into the garage plug. **ABOVE LEFT** Wall fountains come in a dozen different finishes. This traditional terra cotta stands out nicely against the tight lattice privacy screen. Lattice fences are ideal for these since you can thread the cord back through the holes and down the back side out of sight. This fountain is framed by a bent willow and grapevine arbor trellis that is made festive by strands of twinkle lights. Eventually, the ivy poking through the lattice will be trained to frame this fountain as well. **LEFT** The patina of age is a highly valued quality in garden art. The many tones of this cast-stone fountain feature an irregular faux verdigris finish enhanced by further variations due to minerals and algae.

Wall Fountains

The Romans were masters of hydraulic engineering. Ancient homes had some of the first plumbing, and often there were special features built into walls for washing. The Romans were notorious bathers, and their daily ablutions were rarely ignored.

A remnant of this European style can be found at a California historic mission at Carmel, built in the late sixteenth century. In the refectory where Padre Junipero Serra and his fellow brothers dined is a very similar feature. A pipe was inserted through the old adobe wall from the kitchen cistern to the dining room, where a ceramic-lined basin had been built into the wall. The padres would wash ceremonially before taking meals.

The wall fountain in all its forms is the most ingenious means of creating water features in space-starved urban gardens. Michael frequently adds some kind

of framing, be it a built-in feature or a simple prefabricated iron arch. These fountains consist of a back plate that is often quite ornate and contains a spout. This is frequently a lion's head or other motif. The basin is actually half-round and fixed onto the face of the back plate at the bottom. The pump is usually hidden in the basin and feeds a line in which water runs up the back to the spout, where it falls into the basin again.

Wall units are simply hung like a heavy painting from mounting brackets sunk deep into the wall. The plug cord may be routed through the wall or hidden by plants, depending on the means of electrical connection. Water is poured into the basin, you turn on the fountain, and—violà!—instant Roman fountain.

Permanent-Construction Fountains

When the need is for something too large for prefabricated units, or if you're looking for a one-of-a-kind fountain, the only way to go is permanent construction. This is not a place for budget gardeners, but these beautiful works of water art will grab any guest's attention. The sky is the limit here, and some can be as expensive and elaborate as swimming pools. Sometimes it's hard to tell them apart except for the lily pads.

Sometimes you can combine a freestanding unit with a wall fountain when you lack a wall to hang it on. This very unique water feature is well grounded with a wide rectangular base and a vertical arched wall that was no doubt inspired by classical Italian design. Its finish is made to appear very old, and even the discoloration of the water flowing down the face is rustic and beautiful. In time it will develop moss and algae stains that help it blend into the landscape more naturally.

TOP RIGHT This water feature is a hallmark of Glassman design, because not only is it highly attractive, but this concept can also be worked into very narrow spaces such as side yards. It also provides a good backdrop, and behind it tall plants will block out the view beyond. This example is a true water garden and is chemical free. The front wall of the trough has a wide cap, making it a comfortable and convenient seatwall. **TOP LEFT** The back wall rises to 5 feet (2 meters), is faced with cantera stone, and centers on a terra cotta lion's head. It does not extend the entire length of the rear wall of the trough, however, to allow places to use pots such as these fuchsias to flank this taller arch. **ABOVE LEFT** Now the view in its context shows how the waterwork enhances this cheerful rustic outdoor dining area. **ABOVE RIGHT** In the narrow space between window and fence, the Glassman technique of trough water gardens fits in naturally. A step-up back wall of cantera stone frames a bronze boy with fish sculpture and spout. Black bamboo rises above to screen off the neighbors. Such close inspection requires turquoise waterline tile to keep the moisture from wicking up into the stone above and staining it. There are many kinds of containers for water lily roots, but this terra cotta urn is a perfect choice.

ABOVE For a more modern effect, fountains can be spare and as subtle as this black granite column polished to a glassy surface that gleams with wetness. The house presented this tall footing to the outdoor patio—so to transform a potential eyesore, it was veneered with Indian slate which serves as a muted backdrop for the geometric granite. **LEFT** Though this seems a pricey custom design, it is really very simple. The reservoir is buried underground and filled with stones. Then a ring of irregular black slate is mortared securely in place. It is at once contemporary and primitive, surrounded by ferns.

A simple koi pond water garden on a flat site makes it a natural component of this semiformal perennial garden. The relationship of the bench is crucial in that it forces the user to gaze in the desired direction. It also receives enough sunlight each day to support a variety of water plants.

ABOVE LEFT Natural pools can be built to bring the user much closer with cantilevered wood decks. **ABOVE RIGHT** This pool, over ten years old, provides a habitat for the owners' exotic waterfowl. The beaches show no sign of concrete, yet the entire pool is made of gunnite. Careful placement of every stone is required for such a seamless effect.

Water Gardens *Au Naturel*

By far the most difficult kind of fountain or water feature to build is a natural one. In the wild there are powers that shape riverbeds, lakes, and shorelines into their unique wild perfection with no two places on earth visually identical. The Japanese have studied exactly what makes up the natural rock formations and the arrangement of boulders; they have honed it to a fine art that we in the West will never truly understand, but we can learn from our own experiences.

You may perceive the beauty of nature as a single composition. A painter may see the same view as an assembly of varying colors and light. To a landscape artist, it is a distribution of materials, the stone in all its shapes, be they rounded and smooth or sharp and irregular.

A model for detail of a natural pool can be found in the cross-section of a riverbed, with boulders that force water in one direction or another, perhaps enclosing it for awhile in a slower-moving pool where sand and gravel settle out. All around, the stone sizes relate to the patterns of the river.

ROCKS AROUND THE EDGE OF WATER SHOULD NEVER LOOK LIKE RING-AROUND-THE-ROSY IN A CIRCLE. IN NATURE, EVERYTHING IS IRREGULAR.

—MICHAEL GLASSMAN

Such is the level of detail you must grasp to create a wholly natural effect in a contrived, man-made landscape. It is truly a challenge, and these rules of size and color and arrangement are all crucial to the success of the artifice. When water is added to the picture, we explore the relationships between its edges and landforms, and ultimately the rocks themselves.

The art of creating natural waterfalls and pools is a challenging one when you consider the mechanical requirements. To do it in a tiny space is even more difficult, but certainly achievable for the critical eye and the patient hand.

ABOVE LEFT Before the new planting grows in, you can see the skeleton of this remarkable little water garden. You enjoy a rare glimpse of the new gunnite bottom in this first pool, along with the cap for the drain. It will be disguised by a lining of stones. Great moss boulders were set at the edge, and the concrete patio was poured right up to them, then covered with Indian slate. This is an excellent masonry detail that is both dramatic and maintenance free, plus it adds extra seating. Ornamental grasses and variegated *Liriope muscari 'Silvery Sunproof'* will combine with lavender and cool-colored groundcovers by next season. **ABOVE RIGHT** Using natural river-rounded cobble provides a smooth transition from one elevation to another. The stones must be carefully placed to avoid any view of the liner or concrete channel underneath. A water feature such as this must look good whether it is running or not.

Filtration

Always include some kind of filter system with permanent water gardens. The overall goal in water quality is to keep nitrogen levels low to prevent algae bloom. Nitrogen is a by-product of organic material decomposing in the water. Both plants and fish produce such material, and the nitrogen then stimulates algae, resulting in water that's green and cloudy.

The filter should be operated by a smaller pump that is separate from the main waterfall or fountain pump. The reason is that the filter should run all the time, not just when the fountain is flowing, so that you ensure consistent water quality. If you live where there is a lot of dust and other windblown material, consider a larger, more broad-spectrum filter designed to pick up particulate matter in the water as well as nitrogen.

Biofilters are highly recommended for natural water gardens with plants and fish. The unit is packed with straw, sand, or other material to create an ideal environment for certain bacteria that feed on nitrogen. As the water is slowly pumped through the filter, the nitrogen is consumed by the bacteria. It is important to run the filter daily, because if it is allowed to dry out, the bacteria populations inside die quickly, and it will take time to build back up to the previous level of efficiency.

Glassman's Rules for Successful Natural Pools

1. Always use real stones, not the manufactured ones that look bad after awhile.

2. Always avoid the rock-on-water look—it should be rock-in-water.

3. Use concrete and mortar sparingly, because they ruin the natural beauty of rock.

4. You must never see the source of the water.

5. Never allow concrete, pipe, or liner to be visible—always cover with cobble or flagstone without mortar.

6. Always use rock that is indigenous to the area so it never looks out of place.

7. Vary the sizes of rocks as much as possible.

8. If you use a plastic liner, be sure it is completely covered for a better look and to extend the life of the product.

9. Always provide a way to drain the pond without the need to siphon it out for cleaning. Otherwise, it will soon turn into a planter when you get tired of sucking on hoses.

10. If you want pretty water, use chlorine.

Other Tips from Michael

The best way to gain a feel for how natural water features should look is to go out into nature and study them. Contemplate the lay of the land as it relates to water, because there is a critical connection between the two. Notice stones in and around streambeds for their sizes and locations, because there is a certain logic to their natural arrangement. Study what kinds of plants grow in the water, and how those around the edge transition to the dry environment.

Water is a medium, just like soil, and water plants respond the same way as land plants do. Too much nitrogen in the soil, and plants grow very quickly; too much nitrogen in the water and algae grow like crazy.

Make your pool easy to clean—that way, if you go on a trip and come home to green, slimy Jell-o, it won't be a disaster.

The catch-22 is that water lilies (*Nymphaea*) need a lot of sun to grow. Algae requires sun, too, so the exposure that is desirable for a blooming water garden is the same exposure that threatens water quality. Shady water gardens never bloom, but rarely suffer algae problems, either.

Drains

It is recommended that you drain, clean, and refill a water garden at least once a year. If the pond is located on high enough ground, you can use a gravity drain. Simply open a valve, and the water drains away. If your water feature is situated on ground too low for this method, which is often the case, a pumped drain system is required.

You don't have to drain your pool like a bathtub if you have a waterfall or circulating pump. Install a special three-way valve in the supply line. This fitting has an entry port and two exit ports, each with its own gate valve. One exit port feeds your waterfall, and the other is a discharge port that remains closed except when draining the pool. You should have a hose attachment for the discharge port so that when it's operating, the water doesn't spray out right at the opening.

When pumping out the pond, attach the hose to the discharge port. Close the gate valve to the waterfall port and open the valve on the discharge port. Turn on the pump, and it will quickly evacuate all the water. If, when planning your water garden, you're unsure about the need for a waterfall, remember that it works as a drainage mechanism, as well.

Water lilies (*Nymphaea*) don't ask for much more than at least four hours of sunlight per day and a nice, shallow pool to live in.

Though they can grow in lower light, they may not bloom reliably.

On Plants and Fish

The art of water gardening is a quest to achieve a perfect balance of plants, fish, and algae-consuming organisms such as snails. In an ideal world, the fish eat plant residue and algae eaters consume the nitrogen from fish excrement. This is the key to sustainable water quality, but in the real world it can be a difficult condition to achieve without the help of a biofilter.

Water gardens for koi must conform to a few basic guidelines. To support koi fish, the pool must be at least 3½ feet (1 meter) deep. Although other kinds of fish will live happily in more shallow pools, this makes them highly accessible to cats, raccoons, and other predatory wildlife. Always include a ledge, bridge, rock, or other element in or over the water to provide a shady place for the fish to hide and keep cool on very hot days. Water lilies and lotus plants have depth limitations, too, although you can put their root containers on overturned pots or other pedestals to bring them up to the proper location.

There will be a certain degree of maintenance required to ensure the balance remains at desirable levels. Water plants do need fertilizer and repotting from time to time. And you must come to terms with the fact that the clarity of the water will never rival that of a chlorinated pool fountain. There will always be a certain amount of debris in the water, but if you follow these suggestions for care, you can cut down on a lot of common recurring problems.

Make a habit of skimming off leaves and other organic material daily before they settle to the bottom, where they are more difficult to extract. This is a great excuse to relax around your water garden as you leisurely clean the water. At the same time, note the water level and fill it promptly if low. Change the water at least once a year, even if you have a filter, because layers of slime do build up on the inside walls and rocks. Completely drain the pond and scrub all exposed surfaces and rocks with pumice stone or steel wool to remove any slimy buildup.

An Overview of Water Plants

Volumes can be written about plants used in and around water. Here we will simply look at some common species in gardens that are typical of those you'll find at local supply sources. True water garden plants are termed *aquatics* or *marginals*. Aquatics grow in the water all the time, while marginals have evolved to adapt to fluctuating edge conditions of natural pools and river banks.

The beauty of water garden plants is that they are actually grown in pots set down into the water. This allows you to grow very tender, exotic plants that can be brought indoors for the winter.

Hyacinth Nitrogen Barometer

The best and simplest way to gauge the amount of nitrogen buildup in your water garden is to use the common water hyacinth, which can be purchased at any water garden supply store. Place the plant in the water. If it turns yellow in just a couple of days, your water is fine. If the hyacinth stays nice and green, though, you've got way too much nitrogen in your water. You will have to adjust the balance of fish and plants, or replace the water entirely to start over. To rescue the hyacinth for testing again in the future, take it out of the water garden and place it in a bucket of fresh water. Add a tablespoon of water-soluable houseplant fertilizer to the water and mix well to green up the hyacinth, and place in a sunny location.

ABOVE LEFT Graceful papyrus reeds (*Cyperus papyrus*) are the most beautiful reed plants for gardens. They are, however, quite frost tender and cannot live outdoors year-round in any but frost-free climates. **ABOVE CENTER** The prehistoric horsetail reed (*Equisetum hyemale*) is a small-scale alternative to bamboo. It has different kinds of growth—sometimes the reeds are smooth, and at other times in their life cycle they develop these whorls of needles, from which comes another of its common names, *bottle rush*. **ABOVE RIGHT** This semiaquatic iris (*Iris ensata*) is the most colorful of marginal plants. These Kempheri hybrids are commonly called butterfly iris because the flowers sit atop the reeds and flutter with the slightest breeze. A blooming mass such as this has been likened to a flock of butterflies alighted on the plants.

Blooming Aquatics

The reigning queens of the water garden are water lilies and lotus, which are often confused yet are very different plants. The key to identification is the leaves. Water lily leaves lie flat on the water like the lily pads you see in old cartoons. Lotus leaves sit on rigid stems above the water at varying heights. Lotus require a much bigger soil mass to grow than water lilies do, which eliminates their use in very small water gardens. But the beauty of the lotus that so captured the Far East makes it a highly favored plant.

Water lilies are sold in a huge variety of hybrids and flower color. Their hardiness ranges considerably as well, with some strictly tropical. Therefore it's important to choose lilies that are hardy in your local environment to avoid any losses to unexpected cold snaps. Water lilies are also planted in pots that sit underwater, and each kind requires different soil masses, depending on its size and preference.

Iris and canna lilies are also found in water gardens, though they bloom only during a limited period compared to the more everblooming lilies and lotus. They grow in pots at the edges of water gardens at depths of just 4 to 6 inches (1 to 1½ centimeters). Iris offers shades of blue and purple not available in lotus or lily flowers. The canna lily grows at a depth of 6 inches (1½ centimeters) and even when not in bloom, its wide, succulent leaves lend a decidedly exotic character to the water garden.

Reeds and Marginals

There are a few classic reeds that are frequently grown in water gardens due to their ease of cultivation and unique characteristics. The genus *Cyperus* includes two very popular plants: the Egyptian papyrus (*Cyperus papyrus*), which can grow to be well over 6 feet (2 meters) tall, and umbrella palm (*Cyperus alternifolius*), which is not a palm at all but a grass.

Horsetail reed (*Equisetum*), and its many varieties, is actually a very primitive plant, a living fossil that hasn't changed much for millions of years. It is preferred as a water reed because of bright green coloring and segments that make it a much more well-behaved alternative to bamboo.

A dry streambed is the next best thing to a real flowing stream. Whenever dry streambeds are used in a landscape, the goal is to create the illusion of water. This is done by careful arrangement of the stones as they would be in a wild natural stream, whether flowing or not. The flowline, or center of the stream, is usually lined with the smallest stones to create a sense of continuity. Reed-like plants are also worked into the edges to suggest water, as this relationship is universal.

The real illusion, however, can be created at night through lighting. The trick is that the light must shine on a horizontal plane rather than up or down. This highlights the flowline of the streambed by carefully contrived light and shadow. Twelve-volt lights are ideal for this application because you can easily move them around for just the right effect.

Station the fixtures at intervals along the entire length of the streambed shining into the center from both sides alternately. Arrange the rocks around the fixtures themselves so they are not visible by day, leaving a sizable opening in front of the bulb so it can shine out. Wait until dark for the final adjustments of the lights. You will be very surprised how light behaves a lot like water; and, like a real water-filled stream, you can manipulate this one to mimic nature in a sinuous, fluid way.

This dry streambed is a perfect example of how stones are arranged in stream condition with or without water. The shadows show here how light bounces off the larger stones, while the low spots where water would naturally sit remain darker. There are enough stones here of many sizes to hide the light fixtures and make this streetside landscape come alive at night.

Irish moss (Sagina subulata) isn't a true moss. It's a ground-hugging plant that is thicker than moss and is most often used in and around stones in dry streambeds or rocky outcroppings. The contrast between the bright green moss and pale rock creates much more visible drama. Dry streambeds such as this often disguise drainage inlets, French drains, and flowlines hidden underneath the stones.

Water Wisdom

After exploring the life and magic of water in the landscape, it's difficult to contemplate a garden without some kind of fountain or pool. This has become the single most pervasive element in Michael Glassman's work, for its variations are unlimited and its effect is timeless. What the ancient Egyptians knew millennia ago, we are rediscovering in a world of technology that is making water gardens a distinct possibility for every garden and every gardener.

Whether you simply hang a wall fountain on your patio or install a large, fully fitted water garden, the result will be charming. But remember the details discussed here and the importance of nightlighting to maximize the drama of water. Don't forget the need for pumps and filters and the ability to control your water without ever stepping outdoors. Above all, know that water is the most rewarding and animated living amenity you can add to your garden.

CHAPTER 7

ENCLOSURE IS DESIRABLE WHERE PRIVACY IS DESIRED. . . .
IT HAS BEEN SAID THAT, IN OUR MODERN CIVILIZATION,
PRIVACY IS AT ONCE ONE OF THE MOST VALUABLE AND
ONE OF THE RAREST COMMODITIES.

—JOHN ORMSBEE SIMONDS,
LANDSCAPE ARCHITECTURE, 1961

Security and Privacy

The Search for a Secluded Oasis

SENSORY OVERLOAD. IT IS A SYMPTOM OF TOO MANY PEOPLE, TOO much visual information, and a life that is moving too fast. Yet we cannot withdraw from society; we must learn to contend with the daily onslaught without sacrificing too much of ourselves in the process. Our greatest consolation is the fact that we might find a place set apart, an environment into which we may withdraw for periodic renewal.

In recent years, the term *cocooning* has been coined to describe a trend where people prefer to stay home to socialize, entertain, or enjoy hobbies rather than go out to public places where traffic, crowds, and the threat of crime diminish the pleasure of these experiences. Violent crime and gang activity, once perceived as urban problems, have now appeared in suburban areas. People are reacting with insecurity, causing many to reexamine the function of their own back yards. Where once, certain home improvements weren't cost effective because public parks and other areas could be enjoyed for free, now homeowners are reevaluating these costs as public areas become vulnerable to gang activity, drive-by shootings, and child predators. Practical concerns such as insufficient parking and safe restroom facilities are also a factor.

What the need for privacy and the fear of crime have done is to make it worthwhile to put more money into improving your back yard than ever before. Homeowners are achieving this in myriad ways, depending on the number of children, preferred sports, and amount of land available. In addition, the concerns for security are placing greater emphasis on barriers and visibility to discourage intruders. Therefore the issue of security and privacy are closely linked to enclosure and separation, be it physical or visual.

The Elements of Privacy

The creation of a private garden in the city is actually a problem-solving process. Cities all share the same characteristics, so the ideas developed by landscape architects to reduce or disguise the problems can be applied just about anywhere. The only changes may be with materials and more locally adapted plants. Consider these as the fundamental challenges and how they are dealt with.

Privacy is primarily a visual perception. It has to do with who sees you and from what vantage point; nobody can really feel wholly relaxed if they know they are being observed. You probably have an idea of where your privacy problems usually occur. Most often it is caused by your next-door neighbor's house, where second story windows have a bird's-eye view of your entire yard. Problems can also occur on the ground plain from adjacent land uses such as streets, parking lots, and even parks.

The only true way to solve such privacy problems is through enclosure. This may occur on one or more sides of the space, and sometimes overhead too when multistory buildings are involved. There are some simple, effective ways to increase back yard privacy, each with its own benefits and liabilities.

Plants

The beauty and low cost of plants make them the best choice for increasing privacy. Planted close together, they can act as living walls that offer tremendous interest for every season and a pleasing green color to soothe the eye. The only drawbacks are that plants can take years to reach maturity and achieve their optimal function. And, as living things, they have an increased vulnerability compared to hardscape barriers. If one plant dies or if the whole stand is neglected, the entire thing dies and you instantly lose the screening benefit.

Nothing is more natural to look at than plants, and they do the job without giving you the feeling that you are hemmed in. Green is considered the most pleasing color to the human eye, and there are in fact more shades of green than any other color in the spectrum. The key to success is to choose the right plant that requires no special care and is as well adapted to local climate as possible. The second half of the equation requires you to plant at close spacings so they fill in as soon as possible, often before they have fully matured. This also makes it easier to repair a screen or windrow if a plant dies, so there is as small a gap as possible to fill with a new one.

Property line screening applications also occur in tandem. Evergreen trees are perfect along property lines when planted as *windrows*. A windrow is simply a single row of trees planted close together, as farmers do with windbreaks to protect crops. Trees can exceed the height of a neighbor's second-story view, making them the perfect solution, but they don't screen well on the ground-floor level.

The second level occurs on the lower level, where visibility by ground-floor windows or passing pedestrians and motorists requires a second strata of planting. Trees rarely keep their ground-floor foliage, so you will have to plan if you have no fence behind or a transparent one.

Some people are not willing to sacrifice precious sunlight for privacy during winter, and therefore use deciduous trees instead. These are better suited to passive solar design, particularly if located on the south side of the house. They shade the house in summer to relieve your air conditioner or cool things off if you don't have one. In winter, the barren trees cast only the shadows of their branches and allow the weak sunlight to naturally warm the outside walls and brighten the interior through windows. The only disadvantage is that you lose your privacy screen temporarily.

Trees for Back Yard Privacy

The following table features trees that adapt well to windrows, providing a good screen from second-floor windows.

Botanical Name	Common Name	Type	Foliage
Abies concolor	White fir	Needled	Evergreen
Cupressus sempervirens	Italian cypress	Needled	Evergreen
Eucalyptus spp.	Eucalyptus	Broadleaf	Evergreen
Ilex aquifolium	English holly	Broadleaf	Evergreen
Laurus nobilis	Grecian laurel	Broadleaf	Evergreen
Liquidambar styraciflua	Sweet gum	Broadleaf	Deciduous
Picea glauca	White spruce	Needled	Evergreen
Pinus sylvestris	Scotch pine	Needled	Evergreen
Podocarpus macrophyllus	Podocarpus	Broadleaf	Evergreen
Populus nigra 'Italica'	Lombardy poplar	Broadleaf	Deciduous
Sequoia sempervirens	Coast redwood	Needled	Evergreen
Taxus baccata	English yew	Needled	Evergreen
Thuja occidentalis	Eastern arborvitae	Needled	Evergreen

A difficult house on a difficult lot presents the greatest opportunity to create enclosed privacy using constructed materials. An elevated wood deck designed onto the end of the house fronts on the street facing west toward the sunset. The entire deck is enclosed by a louvered fence, and overhead is a shade structure that maximizes shading in the hot afternoon sun.

Shrubs for Back Yard Privacy

Botanical Name	Common Name	Type	Foliage
Cotoneaster lacteus	Parney's cotoneaster	Berries	Evergreen
Euonymus japonicus	Euonymus	Broadleaf	Evergreen
Juniperus spp.	Juniper	Needled	Evergreen
Ligustrum texanum	Texas privet	Flowering	Evergreen
Nerium oleander	Oleander	Flowering	Evergreen
Photinia × fraseri	Toyon	Flowering	Evergreen
Prunus laurocerasus	English laurel	Flowering	Evergreen
Pyracantha coccinea	Scarlet firethorn	Berries	Evergreen
Rosa rugosa	Japanese rose	Flowering	Deciduous

Fences

Fences are instant privacy screens, but you will be limited as to their height if you want to build along the property line. Building codes keep them around 6 feet (2 meters) tall, and although it's possible to apply for a variance, this is a costly and time-consuming process that should be reserved for really difficult situations. One of the most interesting ways to get around this is to take advantage of the fact that the rules only apply to fences on the property line. If you build another barrier inside the perimeter fence, the rules may no longer apply.

When creating fences for privacy and screening, there are great advantages to using semitransparent barriers rather than solid ones. The ability for light and air to pass through the barrier makes it more conducive to plant life and doesn't cut down on your visual space so completely. Popular materials for these applications include wood or plastic lattice and bamboo. The degree of transparency can vary considerably, but an equilibrium must result between openness and privacy.

LEFT Inside the new outdoor living area it is light and airy, and although this is a fully enclosed space, there is no sense of being fenced in. The glimpses you see of sky and the dry landscape beyond are strictly controlled so that no excess hot sun will penetrate in the late summer afternoon. Ceiling fans increase the livability of this space, and the raised planter adds a gardenesque character without using vines that must be pruned and trained. BELOW LEFT Lattice seems to be the single material in the garden world that is universal and never out of style. Today, you can choose wood lattice that is standard material or heavy duty. Heavier woodwork extends the life of the lattice considerably. The sizes of the holes vary, and the grid may be square or on a diagonal. When you apply white lattice onto a dark background, it is more highly visible than this example designed to make the green and red bougainvillea vines stand out more crisply. BELOW RIGHT Over time, lattice planted with vines such as this star jasmine (*Trachelospermum jasminoides*) may become entirely cloaked in foliage. This makes them appear more like a hedge than fence.

The new used brick patio was built like an extension of the interior rooms. It was laid in a herringbone pattern with brick ribbons along the edges. The planters around the edges help take up grade more conveniently. The seatwall at left was created to eliminate the need for a safety railing, and at the same time reduce the need for patio furniture. It is abnormally wide, which increases comfort, allows custom-made cushions to be laid on top when entertaining, and even offers a great place to lie down for an impromptu catnap. A barbecue center makes for more convenient outdoor entertaining now that it can back up to the fence.

Profile: Fern Dell

The greatest benefit any landscape designer can hope to encounter is the existence of old specimen trees. Trees, with their great age and ability to completely transform a place by their mere presence, are the pivotal element in design, for they cannot be moved or altered in any way. Their priceless beauty is such that they govern the entire landscape.

Such was the only amenity worth saving in this garden in an old neighborhood where towering street trees shade the avenues and in the rear yard are similar specimens. The old landscape had become overgrown, making the big redwood tree in the far back corner disappear into other foliage. An old wood deck served as a back patio, and a wisteria-shrouded shade arbor produced a very dark cavern off the sliding glass door. This stepped down onto a broad lawn, and the entire site opened onto the detached garage at the rear of the lot and the adjacent concrete driveway with the neighbor's two-story house just a few feet beyond.

WE HAVE NOTHING TO FEAR AND A GREAT DEAL TO LEARN FROM TREES, THAT VIGOROUS AND PACIFIC TRIBE WHICH WITHOUT STINT PRODUCES STRENGTHENING ESSENCES FOR US, SOOTHING BALMS, AND IN WHOSE GRACIOUS COMPANY WE SPEND SO MANY COOL, SILENT AND INTIMATE HOURS.

—MARCEL PROUST, *PLEASURES AND REGRETS*, 1896

The key to the project was to create a patio of the same quality as the house—a great example of 1930s European-inspired architecture. Brick had been incorporated into the front entry, and it was carried through so that both areas together provided a sense of exterior continuity. A secondary material—Nevada moss flagstone, a poor relative of slate—was applied to footpaths and divider strips. In the rainy season, its nooks and crannies sprout mosses that add to its rustic character. This paving material is more natural and easily integrated into the planting areas than rigid brick.

The second major improvement was to increase security and improve privacy. A screen fence was designed to be an attractive barrier to close off the garage and driveway, plus as much of the neighbor as possible. It does a great job of enclosing the garden so it no longer is associated with the vehicular area. Since it is inside the property lines, the fence height was not constrained by building codes and could be built to 8 feet (2 meters) tall. What does affect it, though, is the scale— any higher, and its mass would overwhelm the garden. So its height was designed like that of a shade arbor, so that the overhead beams would be naturally in scale with the average person. The fence manages to screen off all of the neighbor's house except for one window near the roof peak.

The garden itself would retain its original woodland feel, using the preexisting redwood tree and the weeping Japanese cherry to produce the skeleton of the landscape. The planting was sorted through, and much of it was removed to allow space for new perennials and ferns that would be bright, offering greater variations in texture and color. A narrow space behind the garage was made a storage area for firewood and other odds and ends. A strip of flagstone connected the main patio and new gate, with a hidden utility area out behind the garage. It also linked up with the arbor swing on the far side.

TOP LEFT You cannot build raised planters up against your building walls without risking damage. Moisture travels through masonry easily and will move into the wall and cause serious damage. The term *wicking* has been given to the tendency for plaster and stucco to act like a sponge and draw water upward, and damage can occur to areas where there is no connection if moisture starts making its way up the wall. Rather than take the risk of using waterproof membranes and sealers to block moisture movement, Michael prefers to do away with the connection altogether. He allows an inch or two (less than 5 centimeters) of clear space between house and planter, so small you'd never notice. It is not necessary where the patio abuts the door threshold. **TOP RIGHT** This side of the patio opened toward the other neighbor, who had a clear view of the hot tub after the oppressive vines were removed. To reestablish privacy, a separate screen fence was erected here showing the lattice before it is painted to match the other fence. Because it is part of an overhead structure attached to the house, it ceases to be considered fence, so there was no problem with extending the lattice up to ceiling height. **ABOVE LEFT** The flagstone walk that connects to the back of the garage illustrates one of the most valuable design techniques that take advantage of people's natural curiosity in gardens. A path leading to someplace out of sight beckons us; we want to follow it to its destination simply because it exists. **ABOVE RIGHT** What was originally the ugly backside of the neighbor's garage becomes a perfect surface for white lattice. The white iron bench and dainty bronze lighting fixtures are decidedly feminine, as is the planting composed of various hosta varieties in bloom, impatiens, the variegated *Liriope 'Silvery Sunproof'* (variegated lilyturf), and both babytears and *Campanula poscharskyana* (Serbian bellflower) as groundcovers.

LEFT Another flagstone path leads to the focus point of the garden, where the great redwood tree trunk is exposed and highlighted by this white garden swing. In the planter before it is a small bronze fountain to attract birds to the dozen nesting boxes and feeders scattered about the garden. Lights on the path and small bullets attached to the posts of the swing ensure that this corner of the garden is beautifully illuminated after dark. Without such lighting, night makes gardens disappear into the gloom; but when well lighted, gardens invite you to enter, and inspire a unique feeling when viewed from indoors. **BELOW LEFT** Another way that Michael takes advantage of the power of surprise is in deep-planting areas that would otherwise be little more than a pretty picture. Here he has added stepping flagstones to lure you off the main walk to appreciate the hidden treasures at the back of the bed. Stones make it much easier to fill the bird feeders without stomping on plants or getting muddy. **BELOW RIGHT** The new lattice screen fence that separates garage and driveway from the garden is more complex than it appears. Very solid, it will last indefinitely in part because the lattice is heavy gauge and the holes small. This is a great example of square lattice which can be easy to build because you don't have to cut on the diagonal.

Little decorations mean a lot in small spaces. A whimsical hummingbird on a long stake transforms a simple pot of flowers into an artistic statement.

The overhead arbor did not change; only the vines were removed to allow more light in. Once the foliage was removed, rain came through the arbor right at the sliding glass door, which proved a nuisance. To solve the problem, a sheet of transparent plexiglass was added to the top of the arbor at the door so it would shunt water away and protect the interior floor and window.

This little woodland landscape is not particularly flashy, nor is it created with extraordinary materials. Brick, wood, and a little stone are all that define it, along with a palette of shade-loving trees and flowers. It illustrates that simplicity is the best course to take, rather than forcing a different character on the space. Its traditional scheme is perfectly matched to that of the house and its interior.

This is a garden of enclosure by screen fences, structures, and a dense bank of plants. It highlights the importance of living spaces and the need to have something well defined to catch our interest. Small embellishments used in a big way make the landscape unique for the owner and add to the sense of ownership or attachment. Best of all, it is simple to care for and to live in during the long days of summer, when a cool, moist place is our own oasis in the desert of the city.

Understanding Vulnerability

Every home has a different degree of vulnerability to intruders. In general, intruders prefer homes that are easy to get to by car or on foot. They like an easy access and will choose windows that are not immediately visible from the street. They also avoid houses that are well lit, particularly with outdoor lighting, and those with fences that are difficult to climb over.

The most vulnerable homes are those that back up to alleys or commercial land uses. These provide intruders with convenient parking where they won't stand out, and convenient access over your back fence. Ensuring your fence is well built and without gaps is important, but you can make it downright hard to get over by planting bushy barriers of thorny plants. It won't necessarily eliminate intruders, but it is a big discouragement.

Walls are also great security when living in neighborhoods where there is some gang activity. The fear of a stray bullet is a real concern, evidenced by the number of people indoors who have been killed by drive-by shooters. Remember that concrete block, poured concrete, and stone walls are all virtually bulletproof and therefore add another safety feature.

Thorny Barrier Plants

Agave americana	Agave
Berberis spp.	Barberry
Bougainvillea hybrids	Bougainvillea
Carissa grandiflora	Natal plum
Ilex spp.	Holly
Opuntia spp.	Prickly pear/cholla cactus
Pyracantha coccinea	Firethorn
Yucca spp.	Yucca
Most roses, especially climbers	
Most cactus	

Profile: Territorial Imperative

The term *compound* is defined as "an enclosure containing living quarters, especially in the Far East." In that part of the world, two factors—war and desert—establish the need for such enclosures. Where multiple generations of the same family live together, their combined residences require protection and are built like a fortress, with walls and buildings separating the safe zone inside from aggression outside. Heat, wind, and blowing sand are separated from living spaces by walls as well. A residential compound is more accurately described as a small familial village protected from the outside world.

BY ITS VERY NATURE, THE SINGLE-FAMILY HOUSE IS ITS OWN STATEMENT OF TERRITORIAL CLAIM. IT HAS DEFINED OWNERSHIP BY THE VERY ACT OF ITS POSITIONING ON AN INTEGRAL PIECE OF LAND BUFFERED FROM NEIGHBORS AND PUBLIC STREET BY INTERVENING GROUNDS. AT TIMES THE BUFFER IS REINFORCED BY SYMBOLIC SHRUBS OR FENCES, AND IN OTHER CULTURES BY HIGH WALLS AND GATES.

—OSCAR NEWMAN, *DEFENSIBLE SPACE*, 1972

The owner of this home has roots in the deserts of North Africa and brought to America a love of sun and gardens that evolved from the compounds of Arabian sultans. Their ancient landscapes were an attempt to re-create the verdant, water-filled Paradise as described in the *Koran* (Qur'an Muhammad, XLVII:15), a dream of liquid refreshment to peoples who lived amidst an endless dry wasteland of stone and sand:

> *This is the similitude of Paradise which the godfearing have been promised:*
> *therein are rivers of water unstalling,*
> *rivers of milk unchanging in flavor,*
> *and rivers of wine—a delight to the drinkers,*
> *rivers too, of honey purified;*
> *and therein for them is every fruit,*
> *and forgiveness from their Lord . . .*

The underlying concept of a compound is the most important aspect of this landscape. It is an example of how protected a home can be if no part of the building is exposed to the outside world. Guests will never reach the front door unless admitted through the gate, making the landscape a dry moat over which one cannot pass without authorization. This is highly valuable to those seeking security and privacy. It has always been a luxury of the very rich, but here we see a smaller, contemporary application that provides ideas for use in other average homesites.

The house sat in the middle of a very large lot and was little more than a post war ranch that had seen better days. But it was in a very desirable neighborhood, and the owner decided to completely remodel and expand the original house and take advantage of the entire site through enclosure.

The most difficult challenge is to keep a family compound from looking like a prison camp. Let's face it—unless you use razor wire or electric fence, all barriers are scalable by intruders if they really want to get in. More realistically, enclosures are best seen as a deterrent, a visual statement that this is the boundary. This

This berm extends across the whole front boundary of the property topped with a balustrade interrupted by thick posts that give it sufficient mass. It's broken only at the gateway, where matched retaining walls gently curve it around. The trees are fruitless olive, perhaps the signature tree of Mediterranean gardens. The beds are filled with pink Mexican evening primrose (*Oenothera berlianderi*) and an assortment of lavenders (*Lavandula*) and catmint (*Nepeta cataria*). Note the graceful slope that sweeps down to driveway level, and the driveway paving. Though it is entirely concrete, two colors of stain make it appear more expensive than it is. The dark band was simply separated from the main pour by expansion joints, and this technique was used throughout to break up the expanses of paving with accents.

home needed an automobile barrier above all, and the second concern was to reduce visibility.

The solution involved earth berms along the road in front, which takes incredible amounts of material. Because slopes cannot be successfully planted if they exceed a 3 to 1 ratio or 30 percent slope, the height is limited by the width. To gain a few extra feet of height without adding proportionate amounts to the width, a concrete balustrade was added so that there was a visual barrier that was integrated into the earth barrier. The beauty of this technique is that the view of the road and the neighbor across the street was completely screened off without having to build solid fences or plant dense rows of trees that sacrifice precious sunshine.

Berms and Mounds

The earth berms shown here topped by balustrades are good examples of how grading should be done correctly if plants are to live and if it is to look natural. There are not many rules, but those that do exist are very important. Gradients are gauged by rise and run ratio, so if you have a 5 to 1 slope, that means you need 5 horizontal feet (1½ meters) to rise 1 foot (30 centimeters) in elevation. The rule states that plants cannot grow on slopes greater than 2 to 1, and even this is a bit difficult to work with. A more realistic maximum is 3 to 1, and under no circumstances should lawns be planted on slopes greater than this. Too steep, and the water runs off too quickly to support plants.

When considering earth mounds or berms, you must take into consideration the fact that you must go up one side at a given gradient and down the other side

at the same rate. Plus, you must add a relatively flat part at the top so you don't get a point. Before you decide to take on a berm or mound, do some measurements and then calculate how many cubic yards (meters) of fill dirt it takes to make it work. This roadside berm is enormous and must have required many tractor trailer loads of topsoil to complete. Before you decide to change grades with berms or mounds, be certain you know what it takes and that your budget can accommodate the project.

At the break in the front berm, retaining walls were constructed that flank the entry gateway so that the only view of entering traffic is through this narrow opening. The gates open automatically, while a smaller pedestrian gate provides more convenient access for routine maintenance.

One of the most creative aspects of this whole landscape is the driveway. Normally, quality concrete driveways produce a huge amount of glare and show staining over time from motor oil. The entire driveway, along with the patio at the rear has been textured with special stamps. Then, once it was poured and set, it was subjected to an acid wash. These new concrete staining products can be applied to any concrete, old or new, and the color results from a chemical reaction rather than a dye. It is applied in an irregular fashion to produce an almost marblelike quality for pennies over the cost of plain concrete.

The front half of the compound is divided into three parts: the driveway turnaround, a Mediterranean fruit garden, and the entry court. The fruit garden is a dry place, seemingly transported from the Italian countryside with trellised grapes and citrus in huge terra cotta pots that may be moved in the event of extreme cold snaps. Pomegranate, apricots, and other stone fruit are planted around

Outside, the front berm drops down to street level far more abruptly. To ease the transition, a dry stone wall was constructed at the toe of the slope to take up the grade more promptly. It's easy to tell that very little of the interior of the compound is visible to passing motorists except through the gate.

All three parts of the front of the house are shown here. In the foreground is a corner of the Mediterranean fruit garden. To the right of the entry is the walled court off the kitchen. At far right is a glimpse of the dark driveway. The raised planter shown here, planted with a multiple-trunk crepe myrtle (*Lagerstroemia indica*), was added because the front door walk was too bare and seemed more connected to the driveway than the house.

the edges for a visual (and edible) screen. A twisted old cypress tree was carefully preserved through the entire process, making the perfect backdrop for this kind of garden.

At the front door, a second balustrade encloses a small garden off the kitchen doors. The fountain was designed to increase the height of the enclosure and make it solid enough to block the view of the driveway and parked cars. It provided a perfect opportunity for a water garden and fountain bearing one of two exquisite bronze sculptures. It is bounded by a low wall topped in another classical balustrade, the design element that would occur throughout the landscape to unify the character. But what brings all these spaces together are the roses, shrubs, and trees and climbers planted throughout the front landscape. With few trees, this eastern exposure created the perfect conditions for roses, as sun quickly dries dew off the leaves before fungus diseases gain a foothold.

As you pass around the house, through a spacious breezeway and then through custom double gates into the rear yard, you come to a space that is entirely private due to very tall enclosure of the back of the lot. Originally, there was simply a cut slope that would never support planting, so a retaining wall was added

ABOVE This front courtyard faces east and is off the kitchen for outdoor seating on warm sunny mornings amidst the roses. There is no great need for privacy because of the front berm, so this little garden setting can be open to the garden.

LEFT The amount of glare reflected off the building walls will diminish as the creeping fig vines travel over the surface. This little space is indeed an extension of the fruit garden, with kumquats and dwarf pomegranate combined with roses.

ABOVE LEFT Although this lovely bronze fountain is not overtly showy, the trumpet vines peeking over the top of the wall are the key to its ultimate beauty. Over time the runners will cascade down the front of the wall, eliminating the reflected light and providing a more neutral background for this sculpture.

ABOVE RIGHT Bathed in morning light, this path illustrates how natural concrete acid stain is in the garden setting. The wall and gate were created to cover up the pool equipment and conform with the safety fencing requirements for the pool. This great old cypress is a key feature, and the wood by-product mulch in the garden at left is a great way to keep out the weeds. **BELOW RIGHT** The fruit garden is a place of dry sun, crossed by perfectly trellised grapes, the most popular of the newer seedless varieties. Citrus trees are set out in pots, and young fruit trees grow along the balustrade in the background. Eventually they will fill out and increase the visual screening from the road, plus offer a bonus of delicious edibles.

The Damask Rose: A Mediterranean Odyssey

The story of the damask rose is a long and twisted chronicle that inextricably links it to these dry Middle Eastern gardens. All old species roses blossom but once in spring, but what sets the damask rose apart is that it blooms a second time late in fall, but only in warm-winter climates. This and a very potent fragrance made it the most coveted and widely grown rose of ancient civilizations in the West.

Damask rose

It spread out of the Middle East by way of Egypt, although nobody really knows its exact point of origin. There are references to it by early Persian and Turkish writers, and it is depicted in their tiles and pottery; this points to Asia Minor, but some believe its repeat blooming points to the China roses as its ancestors.

The damask rose also found a home in Greek port cities in the Mediterrranean where it was imported with other commodities. Physicians used the rose fruit as a medicine, but the fruit was small and offered very little vital flesh. The Greeks favored damasks above all for their intense flower fragrance, the essential oils were highly valued in the perfume trade.

Romans, consummate rosarians, helped to distribute damasks to the far corners of their empire. Roman gardeners tried to force winter bloom on damask roses, creating crude greenhouses warmed during winter to mimic Northern Africa's climate by filling tubes with hot water. damask roses are most often depicted in the murals and frescoes of Pompeii. Historians believe that the eruption of Vesuvius destroyed all the damask roses of that region, because only a wild species grows there today. By the fifth century, Rome crumbled as barbarians sacked Europe and agriculture all but vanished, along with the damask rose.

It was not until Saladin recovered Jerusalem from the Christians in 1187 that the rose cropped up again as the source of the 500 camel loads of rose water with which the sultan is said to have purified the Mosque of Omar after it had been used as a Christian church.

The first evidence of its reintroduction to Europe was mentioned in the records of the legendary Crusades. The name *damascena* is rooted in this history, as it was found in Syria in the vicinity of Damascus. It's generally accepted that returning crusader Count de Brie brought it to France in 1270. Later references in 1544 by botanist Matthiolus stated that the damask rose had been known in Italy for a few years, and in 1580 Montaigne reported finding it at a monastery of Ferrare.

The story of the damask rose illustrates how closely roses are tied to the history of gardens in the cradle of civilizations, the Mediterranean. We have hundreds of varieties to choose from today that bloom continuously and are so resistant to common rose diseases that they require no more care than other garden shrubs. The key is location, location, location, and a realization that roses bear a rugged history and a resilient nature that promises at the end of the second millennium we may grow the very same plant that came out of Egypt a thousand years before the birth of Christ.

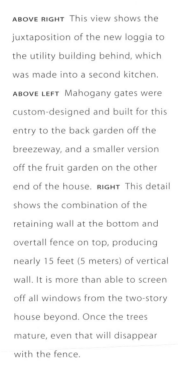

ABOVE RIGHT This view shows the juxtaposition of the new loggia to the utility building behind, which was made into a second kitchen. **ABOVE LEFT** Mahogany gates were custom-designed and built for this entry to the back garden off the breezeway, and a smaller version off the fruit garden on the other end of the house. **RIGHT** This detail shows the combination of the retaining wall at the bottom and overall fence on top, producing nearly 15 feet (5 meters) of vertical wall. It is more than able to screen off all windows from the two-story house beyond. Once the trees mature, even that will disappear with the fence.

ranging from 2 to 4 feet (60 centimeters to 1 meter) tall, which cleaned up this transition rather than struggling to establish plants on that ugly ground. On top of the wall, a fence was built, its height gauged from the top of the wall. Through cooperation, that fence was built even taller than normal; and because the neighbors had no problem with the increase, it was built without interference from the building department.

The main rooms of the house open onto the back yard, and a covered loggia was built on and paved in cantera tile, stepping down to a lower-level cantera paving. This occurs only in this high-visibility area, which looks onto the back of a separate utility building. The wall became the canvas for a raised planter, focusing on a second bronze sculpture fountain that is built into the planter wall.

The remainder of the rear yard space transitions into an open-air patio off French doors at the other end of the house, also paved in the stained concrete. Planting here would be limited to a cool-color palette with occasional bright splashes from bougainvillea or seasonal color. It looks over onto the pool, and a

raised patio is pushed up against the rear yard retaining wall to create interesting changes in grade. For entertaining, this platform provides an area for speakers or musicians that is out of the main living spaces.

This swimming pool was preexisting, one of the few elements that remained during the remodeling. It too was renovated by adding cantera coping stones, cobalt blue tile, new plaster, and an overhead arbor, where a swim bench was built into the side of the pool. Stucco columns, overhead beams, and a backing of grid trellis and a mask-and-urn water feature make this a crucial focal point on a horizontal axis for this long, multiple-space back yard. Eventually it will drip with flowering vines, making it a cool green alcove behind the sparkling turquoise pool.

Although this is a relatively new landscape, its beauty is flowering quickly. Perhaps it is because the design and constructed elements are so artfully arranged that no part of this compound is unattractive. To many it may seem too exposed to the elements, but for sun lovers like roses and grapes, there is no such thing as too much sun. The key is that the landscape itself reflects the preferences of the owner's sense of style and is broadly evocative of his North African past.

What began as a neglected old tract house has been transformed into a Mediterranean villa, from building materials to layout and plants. It is enclosed by visual and safety barriers so that children have free run of the place and parents have lovely patios for entertaining or just outdoor living.

There are elements of ancient Rome here, sculptures reminiscent of the Greek gods and goddesses, and bright colors of tile and flowers to delight and inspire. In the coming years, this landscape will mature and bear fruit in this ancestral compound protected just as in the walled paradise gardens of the Far East.

ABOVE LEFT A view from the elevated patio that fills up the rear corner of the lot. It was preexisting, but the old concrete and brick walls were plastered over to make them appear more integrated into the new scheme. This elevated view of the new arbor and its small water feature shows how it is integrated into the pool swim bench and the retaining wall. New waterline tile, coping, and stained concrete deck tie the old swimming pool seamlessly into the new landscape. This raised planter features a series of matched strawberry trees (*Arbutus unedo*), another ancient Mediterranean plant seen frequently in Pompeiian murals.

ABOVE RIGHT Michael custom-designed this third water feature using white glazed ceramic components. The sensation of water is created most effectively by a tightly contained thin stream. Vines on the trellis are fragrant Chinese jasmine (*Jasminum polyanthum*), and in the foreground is purple barberry (*Berberis thunbergii 'Atropurpurea'*).

The turquoise water of the pool, the cobalt blue waterline tile, the white fountain, and the contrasting grid trellis at the far rear create tremendous contrast to this feature which serves no real purpose except to connect with the pool and break up the long run of fence to the rear. It will no doubt become vital in someone's wedding or party plans in the future.

Make Neighbors Disappear

As with all things, there are extremes. On one hand we have the fishbowl lifestyle, and on the other we live as if under siege. The reality is that our homes are neither public nor fortresses, but a balance of privacy and security. Design is the key to achieving the degree of enclosure we desire, a vision that ranges beyond our own property or yard to take into consideration what occurs on every side.

This desire for a separate place where we may shed the layers of society to rekindle our own fundamental sense of natural freedom is deep in our nature. If that means the ability to sunbathe in the nude, or to fall asleep in the shade without sound and unexpected intruders, the needs are similar. Above all, what is desired is a deep sense of ownership, a kinship with that little spot of land that is your own, where you are free to create whatever reality you wish in order to transcend the difficulties of life in your own urban oasis.

The open, flowing character of this site is evidenced by the natural alignment of the main driveway. The fruit orchard and the balustrade berm act as buffers between the street, neighbors, and intimate morning garden. Such an open layout ensures that all of the planted spaces receive the sunlight they need to grow and bloom profusely. It also allows children lots of smooth pavement for play and a bonus of overflow seating room for large parties.

CHAPTER 8

LANDSCAPE ARCHITECTURE IS INDISPENSABLE FOR LIVING THE
GOOD LIFE . . . IT IS FOR HUMAN ENJOYMENT IN THE 20TH
CENTURY, NOT FOR PROMENADING IN THE 19TH.
—CHRISTOPHER TUNNARD,
GARDENS IN THE MODERN LANDSCAPE, 1938

Site Planning Payoffs

Grappling with Complex Conditions

LANDSCAPE ARCHITECTURE IN ITS BROADEST SENSE TRANSCENDS
gardenmaking with site planning. A site plan is the organized
layout of a particular home or lot that establishes the overall concept of how the entire space is to function. Site planning is crucial in very large homesites, rural land, or where the existing
conditions are so challenging that it is difficult to proceed with
the planting until the large-scale issues are resolved. Lack of experience in site planning is, without a doubt, the most common
weakness found in the landscape industry, because many design

ers lack training in the fundamentals of landscape architecture and engineering.

Site planning requires far more knowledge of mass grading, where the control points exist on the site, how water flows both above and below ground, and the vulnerability of existing vegetation. In addition, one should have a firm understanding of dimensions required to accommodate both people and vehicles, the behavior and erosive potential of soils, and the parameters required for retaining walls and storm drains. The cost to build site improvements today and the potential for liability are so great that there is little room for error on the part of professional or owner.

Site planning is done on different levels depending on the project:

• **Scenario 1:** An unimproved piece of land allows the greatest flexibility, because there are few preexisting constraints beyond those of the topography and vegetation itself. Utilities may be laid without barriers, and the hidden structural changes to the land form are relatively simple as well. At this stage, the designer must lay out how the site is to circulate on both a vehicular and pedestrian level. Then the spaces that are functional, attractive, and connected are incorporated into the circulation.

• **Scenario 2:** A newly constructed home on a still-bare lot requires more care, as there are already some constraints in place. A building pad and site drainage may have been considered. There will be water, sewer, or septic installed that dictate where excavation may or may not occur. Often a driveway is preexisting with access to a garage, and this too directs where and how we create outdoor living spaces. In this case, the work will focus on creation of outdoor living spaces, and areas of practical uses that function well so the site is unified. All proposed improvements must be adapted to the preexisting elements of paving, utilities, and buildings.

• **Scenario 3:** Established homes can be more complex, because you must document all that exists in order to designate what should be torn out and rebuilt in the new plan. These types of projects are filled with surprises, from forgotten utilities to buried foundations. The site planning options are fewer, making conditions closer to traditional landscape design work.

Crucial Control Points

In every landscape, there will be control points. These cannot be compromised and should be considered the most important connections of any new design scheme. If you fail to respond to the controls, the landscape will either fail to function or suffer a variety of practical problems in the future.

Thresholds of doors into the house are primary controls. You can't change the finish-floor elevation of the house, so whatever is adjacent to the threshold must match it perfectly. This connection must often be accurate to a fraction of an inch to protect interior spaces and ensure safety of the occupants and users. If the surfaces are to receive a topping of tile or brick, the thickness of these additions must be considered to set the base slab elevations.

Edges of every constructed element will have to be connected to some part of the landscape. An existing patio slab, driveway, or even street edge sets an immovable elevation that dictates how the sur-roundings are to be laid out. Steps down from an edge must conform to standards, with the first tread from 6 to 8½ inches (1½ to 2 centimeters) below the surface elevation. If the edge is taller than 2 feet (60 centimeters) or so, it may require a safety railing or seatwall (depending on local codes).

Conversely, if an adjacent element is to be taller than the edge, it must also conform to the aforementioned dimensions if it is to step up to a second space or step tread. A very common scenario resulting from failure to respond to controls is when the soil level adjacent to the surface is higher than the slab. Even if the transition is feathered back and sloped, the big problem is that water runs down the higher edge and deposits silt and mud on the surface below. Persistent moisture here can result in algae buildup, creating an unsafe surface for pedestrians.

Foundations of buildings are very important controls that, if ignored, can indeed damage the house itself. Foundations of a typical home are composed of two parts: the footing and the stemwall. Footings are mostly underground, and the stemwall, usually concrete, extends upward from the soil line to the base of the house wall. A "mud sill" of pressure-treated lumber is bolted flat on the top of the stemwall, and the wall studs sit on top of that.

The rule with respect to foundations is that it's OK to change the adjacent grade as long as it does not contact the mud sill. A few inches of stemwall must remain above the soil to ensure that there is no moisture damage. Should soil come near to or touch the sill, it can invite termites, dry rot, wicking of moisture into the wall, and mildew. It will compromise the structural integrity of the entire wall over time.

Trees are serious controls, particularly if they are old, preexisting specimens. Old trees are such a benefit that losing even one can seriously change the charac-ter of a home. All grading must conform to this control point, and engineers set the base elevation for every tree on a site to ensure that their drainage and grad-ing plans conform to these points. The reason is simple—if you mound up soil or gravel around the base of a tree, the bark is denied oxygen, moisture accumulates and the bark rots. This condition is known as *crown rot*. Wherever the bark rots, the cambium layer underneath dies, cutting off the vital flow of water and nutri-ents between leaf and root.

Many kinds of trees are also very sensitive to root disturbance, which estab-lishes a different sort of control. If grading is to be done on difficult sites, the rule of thumb is that soil should not be disturbed within the dripline. This is established by the outside edge of the canopy superimposed on the ground. When cutting and filling for building pads or any other purpose, it's critical that the tree dripline be respected. If not, you may lose the tree quickly or gradually, and all the work you did to preserve it in the landscape may be for nothing.

MICHAEL GLASSMAN

I once consulted on a project where the contractor had mounded soil up against the outside wall of a home. The owners were panicked by mildew and moisture that had ruined the interior wall of the living room. I had to inform them that the contractor had made a serious error by allowing soil to contact the wall, and that not only would the wall require total replacement due to dry rot, but they'd have to tear out the mound and its plants as well. It was all so easily avoidable, and a classic mistake. I *always* leave a gap of at least 1 inch (25 millimeters) between a building wall and any other adjacent improvement.

BELOW This is what greeted Michael when he first came on the job. A small spur in the driveway was meant as a guest entry, leading to the distant door shrouded in shadow. **RIGHT** To create a well-defined sense of entry, a large, heavy beamed arbor was built at the parking spur. Its orientation directed visitors to the path rather than the second drive to the right. The original interlocking unit wall was veneered with wood to match the house, and was heavily planted with flowering perennials and accent trees.

ABOVE Originally the house was dark, and the carport was a chocolate brown that did nothing for the architecture. Overgrown junipers made the parking drab and dull. **RIGHT** The new design began with repainting the house a warm gray and the carport a slightly darker shade. A cloak of young wisteria (*Wisteria floribunda*) vines add bright green color and lavender flowers in the spring. Originally, guests would park here and ascend the narrow, rickety stairway. Now, with the second guest entry, this access stairway is for the convenience of owners or overflow parking.

Profile: The Million-Dollar View

It was built on a tiny pad carved into a rugged hillside that looked east across the crest of the High Sierras. A feat of engineering allowed the house to perch above the abyss, with its swimming pool that seemed to challenge the ravine each time a California earthquake trembled the foothills. Such views are rare, and to build a home like this today would be exorbitantly expensive, making a remodel an excellent investment.

The house was typical 1970s—boxy, natural, with a dozen serious problems that proved a challenge. But the moment Michael Glassman saw that view, he identified the single most tragic aspect of the house. As if it had not been finished, the living room looked out onto all that space, with no way to go out into the fresh mountain air and relax in the sunshine.

The second problem was that it was virtually impossible to find the front door. You would drive up to the stark garage, then search for a small stairway on the left that disappeared into the shaded front door alcove. There had been some attempts to create retaining walls with interlocking masonry units, but the site still lacked an inviting entry and a well-defined guest parking zone. The idea was to make guest parking more visible than the garage, which would require some sizable changes.

GENUINE PLANNING IS AN ATTEMPT, NOT ARBITRARILY TO DISPLACE REALITY, BUT TO CLARIFY IT AND TO GRASP FIRMLY ALL THE ELEMENTS NECESSARY TO BRING THE GEOGRAPHIC AND ECONOMIC FACTS IN HARMONY WITH HUMAN PURPOSE.
—LEWIS MUMFORD, *THE CULTURE OF CITIES*, 1940

The third problem was that the opposite side of the garage driveway dropped off a sheer retaining wall to the pool area, which was hopelessly dated and lacked any areas large enough to use on two sides of the decking. The stunning view of the mountains was on the other side, and the view of the side canyon was literally blocked off by a dense hedge of red-leaf toyon that proved wholly incongruous with the muted surrounding native vegetation.

The owners had plans drawn up to remodel the house by upgrading the interior for more spacious rooms and a balcony added to the outside for better appreciation of the view. But it was designed just 8 feet (2 meters) wide which is far too small to fit a table and chairs. It functioned as a secondary space, when this fabulous view was the very best quality of the entire homesite. Needless to say, plans were quickly changed to a spacious 20 feet (6 meters) wide!

At the time that the deck was scheduled to be built, the cost of redwood had skyrocketed to a point where it was nearly equal to that of tropical hardwoods. With perfect timing, a limited quantity of mahogany became available at the same price as high-grade redwood. This provided an opportunity to use this rare and beautiful material as the highlight of the project.

The new design extended the deck so that it wrapped around half of the house, connecting the entry to a side garden, around the view edge, and back down to the pool. Its dark, rich coloring was oiled periodically to ensure it did not dry out and lose the dark grain.

Another problem with the plan was the railing, a traditional wood affair that gave a fenced-in feeling to both the deck and the view from the interior. With million-dollar scenery, the railing had to meet code but present minimal impact on the

ABOVE RIGHT The new 20-foot (6-meter) wide deck looked out on Clementina Lake with its dam and waterfall, and the north fork of the American River. Simplicity in the deck and railing ensured that no ornate design features would compete with the sublime view.

ABOVE LEFT This detail of the railing shows the cable connections and their turnbuckles. The building code required no more than 6 inches (150 millimeters) between each cable. This is not a good choice for families with small children. **RIGHT** This is the view from the main deck back to the remodeled pool area. It shows the diagonal planking and fine carpentry, plus the contemporary railings, which, when not in the view itself, were constructed of tubular steel rather than cable.

ABOVE RIGHT This view of the original pool illustrates how much area was wasted at the edge and how the hedge virtually cut off the whole space from the beautiful canyon at right. At the far end there was just a simple patio, with no connection to areas beyond. Hot and dry, this old view shows how shabby the original pool area had become. **ABOVE LEFT** Often, simplicity is created by very complex construction; this view from the garage shows the height of the retaining wall just below. On the far side, deck and railing required specially engineered retaining walls and footings underneath. Now the pool is virtually married to the oak-filled canyon beyond. The single poured exposed aggregate deck defines the pool more cleanly so that on the ground plane, where before we saw hedges and coping, Spanish tile and wood deck, we now see turquoise water and a carpetlike exposed aggregate pool decking. **LEFT** Where the tiny patio had barely accommodated a small table and chairs, this new deck provides for spacious poolside dining. Its elaborate overhead was designed to provide a pattern of shade at the time of day it is most needed, and the light-colored stain makes its mass less oppressive. In addition, the wood of the overhead does not compete with the beauty of the mahogany.

Protecting Finicky Oaks and Other Old Trees

Native oaks, particularly in the Western states, are notoriously finicky about what happens around them. The trees germinate and produce a very long tap root the first year to get them through the long summer drought. Years later, the trees develop a system of surface roots that feed off the organic matter in topsoil. Then, when aged, they produce roots between the surface and the tap root.

Many people who are struggling to preserve native oak trees on construction sites know it's a dicey affair. If there is high foot or vehicle traffic under the dripline, the soil becomes compacted, denying oxygen to the roots. Paving around the trees is equally devastating. Changes in grading alter the way water flows on the land in the rainy season, and when there are extensive excavations the subsoil water is also affected. But the greatest threat is water via irrigation, because the trees will not put up with moisture during their dry season.

Moisture fosters the growth of a soil fungus called *oak root fungus*, or *armillaria root rot*. When the soils are undisturbed during the warm months, the fungus is rarely a threat to oak trees. But if irrigation is introduced, the moisture combined with warm soils allows this problem to spread like wildfire.

There are many guidelines available for the protection of mature trees during construction. University Extension offices usually have publications that will help you determine a safe zone around the oak, and find some surface mulches for weed control that are compatible with oak tree needs. If you are planning to preserve an old tree while site planning, it's worthwhile to consult a certified arborist to establish guidelines for your tree. Never forget that the money you pay an arborist is a drop in the bucket compared to the $10,000 value of that beautiful old specimen you so admire.

view. The answer was custom-made tubular steel railings with a series of tensioned cables at 6-inch (150-millimeter) intervals to satisfy the building department. As the cable aged, it would be tightened by a series of turnbuckles. The result was an unspoiled view and a great improvement of the scene from indoors, where a heavier rail would have blocked much of the view.

The swimming pool proved to be a challenge, because the existing retaining walls were unattractive, the pool coping was the traditional old units, and the waterline tile bore a decorative Spanish motif that did not complement the new contemporary design of the site. Therefore the pool was remodeled as well, with new decking overall that would provide one clean pour of exposed aggregate concrete that simplified the whole area and emphasized its geometry.

The new slab would be extended by a second, smaller mahogany deck with overhead shade arbor at one end of the pool. In the brutal summer sun, it was an essential improvement for poolside lounging or dining. The deck cantilevered over the side canyon and provided glimpses of the million-dollar view as well. This is a perfect example of how ground is indeed gained through good design, and what once belonged exclusively to the canyon is now reclaimed by the owners. Though it is perhaps only 10 or 12 feet (2 or 4 meters) out, that is a tremendous improvement that changes the way the entire pool area is used.

The remaining side of the house was changed by the remodeling as well. Originally, this was a forgotten side yard, but the architect's plan called for a new sliding glass door off the dining room to add light to the inside. The strip was difficult, because it was composed of little more than a steep-cut slope and a low swale for drainage, with the finish floor of the house well above grade.

There was enough mahogany available to wrap the deck around the back of the house and through the side yard at about 8 feet (2 meters) wide. It would bridge the gap, allowing drainage to continue unhindered through the swale underneath. A small, natural water garden was carved out of the cut slope, with large boulders added to break up the strip and anchor both plants and water feature. Luxurious foliage plants were added to this oak-shaded oasis, the only truly shady, moist living space on-site.

What had originated as a poorly conceived cliffside residence has been transformed into a perfectly functional and beautiful landscape. No longer is there a question where to park and enter—it's identified by the large shade arbor. With an expansive deck of rich hardwood, the view has become a holistic experience. The pool has been transformed from a 1970s remnant to a stunning contemporary composition. What began as a fixer-upper with a great view is now a million-dollar wonder thanks to an odd lot of mahogany and ground gained by design.

Vehicular Needs

Vehicles of all kinds are part of American life. Accommodating them in a site plan is a high priority that requires some knowledge of the individual user's daily patterns.

Vehicular environments begin with the driveway, which dictates egress to the house and garage. The first priority is to put yourself behind the wheel and imagine how you would drive in and drive out again. The goal is to avoid difficult conditions that require complex turnaround, a long distance to travel in reverse, or overly narrow driveways where the tires can easily drift off the edge and into planting areas.

Aesthetically speaking, driveway alignment should be simple but graceful, with long, sweeping curves rather than sudden corners. It will have a direct connection with the front door, which requires clearly defined, convenient access. There should also be a provision for guest parking if space permits, so that you need not move cars every time a guest leaves.

Parking stalls that you see at the supermarket allow 9 feet (3 meters) in width for the car. You know how hard it is to open your door and get out when the next car is parked off-center; imagine how problematic a driveway this narrow would be. There'd be no paving to step out onto, and with one error your wheel is in a planter or on the lawn.

Plan your driveway at least 10 feet (3 meters) wide if you're tight on space and the distance is short and straight. But if it's a bit longer, or if the driveway curves, 12 feet (4 meters) wide provides greater comfort and maneuverability. This is the width of a standard city street lane, and reduces the chance of an inattentive driver crushing plants and sprinkler heads as tires run off the edge.

The 12-foot (4-meter) dimension allows one car to pass through comfortably, turn, and back up without undue effort. But if you have a long driveway, you may choose to go wider in the event you encounter an oncoming vehicle. If you plan a turnaround that does not require backing up, you must design to the minimum radius, and preferably larger if possible. The drivable surface must be no tighter than 28 feet (8 meters), with over 30 feet (9 meters) a more realistic turning area.

Parking is a big concern, because you are bound to have guests; and if they do not or cannot park on the street, you may want to design for guest parking onsite. There are a few standards you should understand when allowing for parking that are dictated by city codes for the design of parking lots. Although you can manipulate these numbers, it's always a good idea to use the standards to avoid undersizing the area. If it ends up too small to use, you've invested many thousands of dollars on paving that promises to be a source of irritation for years to come.

When you think of a parking space, you can reduce the numbers a bit since the front or rear overhang of a car extends beyond the wheels. Figure 2 feet (60 centimeters) more or less overhang, and avoid planting trees or building anything else that would be damaged by the car bumper in this area. A curb or wheel-stops are used to establish this point and control auto damage of tree trunks.

- A *parallel stall* measures 9 feet (3 meters) by 24 feet (7 meters)—this is on-street curbside parking.
- A *90-degree stall* measures 9 feet (3 meters) by 19 feet (6 meters)—expect to allow 24 feet (7 meters) of backup space to get in and out.

If you must plan recreational vehicle parking, even if it isn't on the driveway, you must use the driveway to get the vehicle stored there. This means that the design must make this possible without giving the driver a headache every time he or she parks the vehicle. When this is a trailer or an oversized motor home, this connection increases the need for turning room. When the RV is behind a fence, it requires a gateway that's wide enough so you have some flexibility when parking. There must be room for a single or double gate to swing open without decreasing your maneuvering room.

Finally, the material used for driveways should be considered, since there are some options. Blacktop asphalt is most common due to its low cost, but its longevity is nowhere near that of concrete. Asphalt requires edging material such as wood header or a concrete strip to keep it in place and looking good over time.

Concrete is expensive, and let's face it—bare slabs produce glare and tend to discolor over a short time, no matter how well they are poured and finished. Tinting has proved a great benefit for driveways because subtle earth tones cut glare and disguise water or oil stains. Exposed aggregate finishes are more natural looking, but expensive. Imprinting is another technique that can really spruce up the look of a dull driveway. No matter what the finish, all concrete requires expansion joints at regular intervals to control cracking. You can beef these up and make them more decorative by using brick, stone, or wood for slightly more expense than a standard joint.

One of the most attractive and affordable solutions is to use more than one material at the same time. Most front entries to homes look better with a higher grade of paving where guests get out of their cars. It's fine to create a field of "good stuff" such as tinted, imprinted concrete at the entry, and then downgrade to tinted concrete or asphalt for the remainder of the drive. Another popular application is to pour a 2-foot (60-centimeter) ribbon down each side of the driveway in a darker color than the center part of it.

The options for driveway design and materials are endless, but if you have young roller skaters or tricycle riders using the driveway, it's best to stick with smooth concrete surfaces that are clean and safe. It is so important to get the size right—if you fail this part, the drive is useless or a perpetual frustration.

No Ambiguous Entries

Ambiguous entries afflict millions of American homes. Sometimes it's the architecture that places the front door beyond more visible forms of secondary entry. Other times, the house is positioned for view or efficiency so that the prominent entry is no longer at a logical point of entry. Either way, guests cannot find your front door and wander around looking for a way to enter. More often than not, it's the utility door where the garbage cans are stored!

The front entry to your home is the most important part of site planning. It is where people come to visit, it's where you hang your holiday decorations, it's the place you welcome friends and family. How people see this entry is directly related to where they are coming from, which may be either from the street or driveway. It is also a major control that dictates how your entire front yard is to be planned and landscaped.

Access should be comfortable in all weather, with convenient parking and a spacious walkway. It should be easy to find in the day, and adequately lighted by night. It's always best to keep paving smooth and simple so female party guests with high-heeled shoes or seniors who might be unsteady on their feet don't struggle. Safety means security for your guests, and reduces any chance for a lawsuit.

A grand sense of arrival makes a guest want to enter. You can achieve this with carefully positioned trees, pilasters, overhead structures, or other constructed elements that literally mark the point of entry so there is no question.

Make the front door area comfortably sized so there will be no crowding. In old homes the porches were so spacious you were not only comfortable, there was likely a swing or arbor where you could wait. Tract homes from the 1960s are notoriously parsimonious with the front door stoop in an effort to save money by sacrificing drama. These are the major offenders, and some modern home styles provide little more than a darkened alcove to mark the entry way.

MICHAEL GLASSMAN

I recommend my clients use a garden hose or kitchen flour to roughly lay out their future landscape on the ground. This makes a big difference in how comfortable they are with the design, and helps identify parts that aren't quite right. It's a lot more affordable to find you need revisions while still on the drawing board than to fill in pools and trenches during construction. Contractors make a surprising amount of extra money on changed orders late in the process.

This is a versatile cooking center featuring a gas grill and a pizza oven. The surfaces are tinted concrete and the stucco masonry is decorated with colorful glazed ceramic tiles for interest. The L shape allows a more convenient working environment and keeps the owners in the middle of the party even while preparing dinner.

Cooking Al Fresco

They are called outdoor kitchens, cooking centers, or just a built-in barbecue. No matter what the name, they mean that host and hostess may prepare meals outdoors without leaving the guests. Today the options and products made for outdoor kitchens are always changing, and, as with an indoor kitchen, you can spend a little or spend a lot.

Consider these various components that are found in today's outdoor cooking centers:

Gas Grill

There has been a virtual revolution in gas grills that may make some of the new deluxe models look even better than your kitchen range. Gas-fired grills that are zone controlled allow you to cook many different types of foods at the same time at their own temperatures.

These sizable built-in units can serve as grill, smoker, and oven. They require a gas hookup, although they are also available in the traditional briquette-fired type. Gas-fired grills are a wise investment, because many cities are banning briquette barbecuing due to dangerous emissions that contribute to air pollution problems. Grills can be purchased in various sizes; for those who entertain extensively, a larger model may be more convenient, making it easier to get all the food out at the right temperature at the same time.

> EATING IS NOT MERELY A MATERIAL PLEASURE. EATING WELL GIVES A SPECTACULAR JOY TO LIFE AND CONTRIBUTES IMMENSELY TO GOODWILL AND HAPPY COMRADESHIP. IT IS OF GREAT IMPORTANCE TO THE MORALE.
> —ELISA SCHIAPARELLI, *SHOCKING LIFE*, 1954

Refrigerator

Although cooking center refrigerators are small, they do save you plenty of trips for refreshments and ice, which can be a burden if your patio area is around a pool distant from the back door. There are special outdoor refrigerator models that are resistant to the weather, but all require an electric outlet.

Sink

If you need to rinse off freshly picked vegetables or simply want a water supply close at hand, these receptacles also allow you to pour spent drinks or other liquids conveniently down the drain. The water supply may offer only cold water, or may include hot water as well. If there is a long distance to the hot water heater, some elaborate cooking centers contain point-of-use water heaters that require electric or gas hookup.

Ovens

A newer additions to outdoor kitchens is the brick-lined oven for baking bread and pizza. These ovens include a smoke stack and come in a variety of shapes. The ovens require wood for fuel that imparts a unique flavor to food.

ABOVE Wood for the pizza oven is stored in the cabinet underneath. First you kindle a fire inside and allow it to burn down to coals. Special hand tools allow you to move the coals around the edges, leaving a clean place inside for the bread or pizza to sit on the heated bricks. A tight half-moon door fits into the opening, and the food bakes naturally until done. **BELOW** It's not difficult to build a fireplace into your cooking center. This beautiful example is highlighted by the vines, which give it better architectural character. Where smoke is a problem, you can add a taller chimney to keep it clear of the living spaces.

Fireplace

On those nippy nights, a fireplace incorporated into the cooking center can make it more cozy to cook outdoors. The fireplace or a similar fire pit may be fueled by gas or wood. It's important to position the cooking center strategically so that the traffic flow is not interrupted, and so it is convenient to the kitchen. There will be a number of trips back and forth, so avoid tricky steps or curbs between the two points. Also, be aware of the position of the sun. Barbecuing is done from around noon until dusk, and if the cooking center is in the hot spot of the garden, you won't be able to change it. Try to position it so that there are shade-giving elements for the late afternoon; but if there's not a lot of flexibility, use market umbrellas to protect the cook. Also, consider its relationship to the adjacent living spaces, because you want to be able to converse freely without having to shout. On the other hand, be sure the center will not cause downwind living spaces undue discomfort from smoke.

Think of materials for the cooking center just as you think of those for the kitchen. The surface will take a beating from weather, so it must be finished in frost-resistant, dense tile that won't stain. Avoid porous materials that suck up every drop of oil you spill. Above all, choose structural components such as concrete block, brick, and surfaces that are coordinated with materials preexisting in the landscape or house.

ABOVE LEFT Placing the cooking center close to dining areas allows you to keep grilling as your guests and family enjoy the food. This intimate setting is ideal for small gatherings. **ABOVE RIGHT** This graceful, crescent-shaped outdoor cooking center is constructed out of the same stone as the accent paving and swimming pool. The dark surface is slate, which resists staining and weathering. The longer side to the right of the barbecue is ideal for a buffet, while the opposite side, with the sink, is a preparation area. **LEFT** Cooking centers can be great problem solvers, and in this garden it provided the ideal end element to balance the patio. The backdrop of white lattice is particularly nice to look at when there is no view. Rather than placing the barbecue in the center, this offset arrangement allows a larger serving area on one side.

ABOVE This photo shows the cross-section of the rear yard. Note the finish elevation of the covered patio. The fence at right is where the setback requirement exists, forcing any construction to begin at least 25 feet (8 meters) back to nearly the center of the space. The oaks on the end of the space were to be preserved as well, setting three controls: setback, trees, and house. This didn't leave much to work with. **RIGHT** The house and office building needed to be connected so that there was a separation between the rear yard and the utility garage spaces. **FAR RIGHT** To comply with the setback requirements and to meet the control elevation of the covered patio, this 4 foot (1-meter) retaining wall had to be created in order to provide as large and level an entertainment area as constraints allowed. This was the original location of the swimming pool that was excavated, then filled in.

Profile: It's Never Too Late

It was a beautiful home positioned on a spacious lot that was bounded on two sides by wild open space of seasonal grasses and oak trees. This gave the rear yard a much greater sense of space than existed inside the fence line. Despite the countrified feel, the rear of the lot was seriously constrained by a 25-foot (8-meter) setback that prevented any construction closer to the existing iron fence. This, combined with a concerted effort to preserve every existing oak tree, no matter how weak and gangly, made the design effort a study in tolerances. These constraints literally cut the usable area in half. The original design called for the pool to be adjacent to the preexisting patio, because that was the only position that would not damage the existing oak trees. But as the pool was dug, the couple realized it was way too close and severely limited the outdoor living space. After much deliberation, it was agreed that a sacrifice of a few spindly oaks was the only way to shift the pool away from the back patio. The old hole was filled in and a new pad for the pool was graded with the addition of a retaining wall to protect the remaining oaks. The new, separate pool area allowed a safety fence to be incorporated into the back yard without cutting off the view of the natural open space through the rear windows.

> NO WISE MAN HAS EVER SAID THAT CHANGE OF PLAN IS INCONSISTENCY.
>
> —CICERO, 43 BC

194

ABOVE RIGHT With the removal of a few small oaks, the swimming pool was pushed to the far edge of the lot. To avoid eating up crucial square footage with a graded slope, this low retaining wall creates a perfect nook for the simple, rectangular pool. The wall also allows the oaks to remain with as much root area as possible. Colorful plantings, cantera stone tiles, and the arbor at the far end give this a semiformal, symmetrical effect that's elegant and simple.

ABOVE LEFT This small Spanish fountain was built into the planters of the raised patio to provide a focal point that is framed by the beautiful woodland beyond.

The final pool design included a beautiful stone column pergola at the far end for a lovely symmetrical alignment with the pool edges. Originally, these beams, as the rest of the woodwork, was painted white, but the owner found there was insufficient contrast against the columns, so they were stripped and painted a warm buttery beige. Similarly, the pool deck was first poured concrete, but they so loved cantera tile used elsewhere that this was changed during construction too.

The new design allowed the back steps to gently transition down to a new main patio. The setback established where the far edge had to be, and there a very large retaining wall was built to keep the new patio on a level plain. This required a tremendous amount of construction, huge footings, and backfilling of the entire area before the topping slab could be poured. The edges included a narrow raised planter, so there need not be a railing that would spoil the view.

The main patio was laid out for entertaining and is very close to the pool so that it is the center of all back yard activity. The cooking center is constructed out of the same blonde cantera stone as the paving. A small Spanish tier fountain was incorporated on one side for the refreshing sound of water on hot afternoons. There is sufficient room for a large table for eight.

Beyond, in the setback area, the original lawn remained for the children's play area. This separation is ideal for family parties because there is a very distinct separation between active play spaces and passive adult zones.

The detached garage and exercise room at the far end of the lot still seemed too separated from the main house. That side of the lot was too exposed and frag-

ABOVE Although it is newly constructed, this colonnaded walkway looks almost like it came from an old European villa. Planted in wisteria vines, the walk is flanked with baroque troughs planted in brilliant flowers. **LEFT** What the landscape doesn't show at this time of year is the careful combination of wisteria and black locust (*Robinia ambigua 'Idahoensis'*). Wisteria is legendary, with its long lavender flowers that will hang down through the arbor. This locust produces remarkably similar clusters of pendulous deeper purple flowers, so that in spring this part of the garden will be breathtaking. Note the simple but legal safety railing that sits outside the columns, rather than being built into them.

RIGHT This lovely little courtyard was created by the new walk. A series of concrete rectangles were poured to connect the back door to the drive-way without sacrificing grass to more paving. The grid trellis on the wall is stained to match all the other woodwork onsite. **BELOW** The front entry to the house is more freeflowing than the rear yard design. A baroque-style tier fountain provides the focal point, and the young roses planted all around the house walls will soon make this view more colorful. The lawn behind surrounds planting islands filled with perennials, fruitless olive trees, and preserved native oaks.

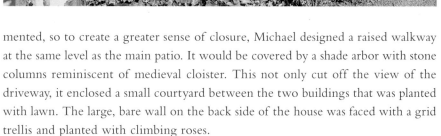

mented, so to create a greater sense of closure, Michael designed a raised walkway at the same level as the main patio. It would be covered by a shade arbor with stone columns reminiscent of medieval cloister. This not only cut off the view of the driveway, it enclosed a small courtyard between the two buildings that was planted with lawn. The large, bare wall on the back side of the house was faced with a grid trellis and planted with climbing roses.

The front yard is more pastoral, with a graceful interlocking paver entry walk that defines a large bed filled with roses that will be trained up onto the building. The trellage added will eventually disappear underneath the foliage and flowers, but what's visible now illustrates how to provide support to plants without damaging building walls and stucco. Roses have stiff canes that must be trained with a certain amount of tension that may strain other kinds of holdfasts directly connected to the walls.

The front yard planting is organized in islands surrounded by verdant green lawn. The islands are designed around existing boulders or oaks that are to be preserved. Islands are always preferable to trees directly in lawns because the grass competes for moisture and nutrients. And with some native trees adapted to dry seasons, the higher water requirement of lawn may spell their demise. Plants were chosen for their compatibility with the architecture as well as the trees, featuring Spanish lavender and a variety of annuals.

Roses were not used in such abundance on the original plans, but after the owners saw what fantastic beauty and versatility there is among this queen of flowers, there was a new direction with the planting. Now this favorite flower fills every nook and cranny of the landscape, and although they are still young, over time the result will be sensational.

ABOVE LEFT This graceful scalloped wall at streetside is planted with dwarf ivy (*Heclera helix*) and a series of grandiflora rose trees. A hedge of shrub roses would have covered up the unique masonry and limited the view of the front of the house.

ABOVE RIGHT It's never a good idea to punch into stucco with nails or even molly bolts, because it provides an avenue for water to enter inside. These simple grids were custom-made for the front of the house, attached to the fascia rather than the wall. It's much easier to train a rose by tying onto the grid than to try to work with smaller supports. Although it is still visible, the roses will soon meet over each window in a perfect arch.

On the far less visible side of the house, there existed menhirlike standing stones that deserved to be highlighted and separated from the air conditioning units.

These plants are a real specialty, and Michael called in a professional rosarian to help choose varieties that are well adapted locally and are proven performers. *Remondance*, the repeat blooming of modern hybrid teas, was what the owners looked for, and they were planted in virtually every form known to rosarians. Rose trees line the driveway. Climbing hybrid teas are newly trained to the fences and walls of the house. Shrub roses serve as foundation planting wherever there is sufficient sunlight. Eventually, all will mature into a riot of fragrant blossoms that so perfectly complement this Mediterranean architecture.

There is, indeed, no sin in making changes to a project even during construction. However, try to get it exactly right on paper because changes during construction are expensive. Rarely is there a change that doesn't have an impact on something else on-site, which can indicate further unexpected costs.

But for many people, the only time they are able to visualize how a project will look is when it is physically laid out on the ground. It is always better to make changes at this stage than to proceed with something you aren't truly happy with. The reality is that you, not the designer, will have to live with the results for a very long time.

In Praise of Planning

The most wonderful part of landscape architecture is that no two sites are the same. Each must be viewed in its own right, analyzed, and designed with response to the needs of the user and the constraints of the site. Because a property is larger, it does not mean that the entire area is buildable or plantable. Precariously steep slopes or the constraints of setbacks and tree preservation can afflict any homesite on a larger or smaller scale. When you understand how the challenges are dealt with by professionals, it lays down a path you can follow in rising to your own limitations.

There's little doubt that building a landscape today is expensive, but there are few things in life that will give you the satisfaction of a beautiful, functional outdoor living area for your home. The constructed elements are the infrastructure that will support all plants and other embellishments, so this is the most critical part of the creative process. If there is one area in which you seek quality regardless of the price, let it be in the hiring of a personable and very experienced design professional. These skills are not learned in a year or ten years, but for the kind of ability evidenced in Michael Glassman's landscapes, it takes a lifetime.

The stones became a perfect place for an out-of-the-way butterfly garden decorated by an Italian tile birdbath. These tall spiked flowers—foxglove (*Digitalis purpurea*), *Acanthus*, bearded iris (*Acanthus mollis*), and Mexican evening primrose (*Oenothera berlanderi*)—are all well-known butterfly and moth nectar sources.

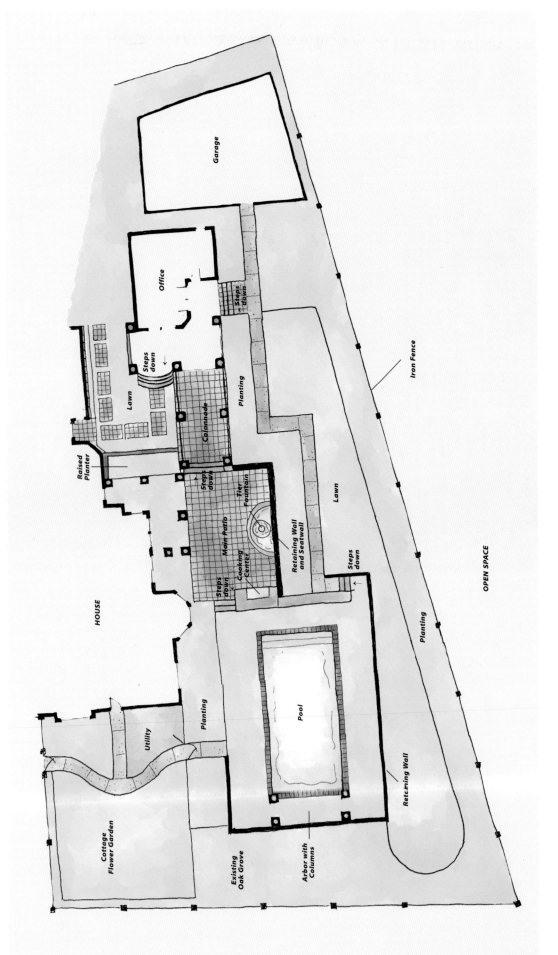

Although this is a large lot, only a small portion of it could be built out. Note how the used spaces are maximized by positioning them very closely to the building to capitalize on the indoor-outdoor spatial connection. The extensive use of retaining walls and judicious positioning of steps sacrifice little ground within the buildable zone. The stepped-back alignment of the retaining wall gains as much ground as possible within the 25-foot (8-meter) setback.